Exploring Oregon

Travel Guide for the Adventurous Wanderer

— *A Maverick Publication* —

ISBN 0-89288-279-4

Library of Congress Control Number: 00-133313

ON THE COVER:
Broken Top in Central Oregon's Three Sisters Wilderness

Cover photograph by Gary Asher

Maps created by Greg Cross

Photographs by Mark Highberger

For additional copies of *Exploring Oregon,* contact:
Maverick Distributors
P.O. Drawer 7289
Bend, Oregon 97708
541-382-2728

Published and printed by Maverick Publications, Inc.
P.O. Box 5007 • Bend, Oregon 97708

To the woman along the trail
with her Labrador retriever.

Acknowledgment

Marc Faulconer of Bend's *The Bulletin* was the first to take a chance on publishing my love song to the state. And every week he lets me sing another verse. Without him, this book would still be only an idea.

Introduction

Oregon. The April blizzard whining and whirring out of Canada washed the word with sleet as I hunkered along the side of Interstate 94 with my thumb out, thinking of home and waiting for the next car to take me one more stretch of asphalt closer to it. But there was a problem: All this sky-domed span of North Dakota pasture stretching on and on to the horizon was empty of cows. In fact, it was empty of horizon. Seems the ranchers herd everything into their barns when the blizzard warning sounds. Hitchhikers, however, are on their own.

"So it's come to this," I said to the road, which lay empty and silent beneath a hovering white cloud. Then the cloud spat at me. I spat back. Though this might be the end, I wasn't going gently into that good night.

Whatever possessed me during America's bicentennial to sell my house in Ontario, store my stuff in Salem, embark on a winter's hitchhiking journey to New York and then a flight to Europe to see what all the fuss was about over there-well, I don't know. But I did know that on this return trip home I wasn't going to take any guff from a North Dakota storm. After all, I was an Oregonian. Joe Meek born and Tom McCall raised. So I girded my loins and gnashed my teeth and waited for destiny to come galloping across the prairie.

"O-O-Oregon," I puffed into my hands, blowing hard to keep my hitchhiking thumb thawed.

Then from far away there came a keening wail. A trumpet blast from heaven? Or a water pump going bad? The wailing faded when an old beige Buick braked to a stop next to me. A window slid down. Two eyes peered through the snow-wash. "Hey, man—where you going?"

"O-O-Oregon."

"Well, I can only take you as far as Portland, but hop in."

I hopped. He drove—90 miles an hour.

From the snow-piled passes of Montana and through the wheat-crested fields of Washington, that beige Buick ran, until it finally bounced over The Dalles Bridge, crossed the Columbia River and jolted down into Oregon.

That's when I leaned over to look out the window. And when I saw white clouds dancing across a blue sky, I wept. No moaning or sobbing, just a quiet, unmanly cry.

"Hey, man—what's wrong?"

"O—" I said. "O-Oregon."

"Sure enough," he said. And we raced along the river, the asphalt humming and the clouds dancing and Oregon all around me.

Oregon, said the sky.

Oregon, said the river.

And I knew I was home. This book, *Exploring Oregon*, is one of the results of that discovery.

Table of Contents

Northwest

Southwest

Central

Northeast

Southeast

NORTHWEST

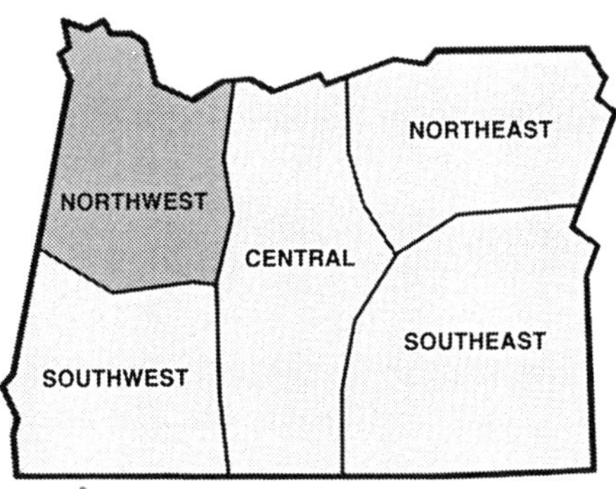

Baskett Slough

In a faraway land where winter is one long night, families of dusky geese fly free each fall for an Oregon river valley. This they have done through years beyond memory—always nesting in Alaska's Copper River Delta, always wintering in Oregon's Willamette Valley. The migration is the same. But the valley has changed.

What sets duskies apart from all other geese is their need for the valley of the Willamette—they refuse to winter anywhere else. But the valley's prairies and marshes and streams began changing as soon as Oregon Trail pioneers began arriving in the 1840s. For more than a century, plowing and draining and channeling created farms and fields and pastures, but it also ruined the duskies' winter home.

Then to this land in the 1960s came Baskett Slough, one of three Willamette Valley National Wildlife Refuges that provide geese with the sanctuary they need to survive the winter, and visitors with an invitation to visit the bird called "king of the waterfowl."

Named for George J. Baskett, an early breeder of thoroughbred horses in the valley, the refuge is located near the junction of Highways 22 and 99W, about two miles north of Rickreall, a crossroads town that once held the annual World Championship of Belly Bouncing. This is still farm land, still flat land, but now its 2,500 acres of fields, hills, and wetlands are planted and diked to maintain a winter home for geese.

For a goose-eye view of it, first drive to the trailhead parking lot (signs clearly show the way), and then hike the one-and-a-half mile loop trail that begins near brambles of blackberry and thickets of oak and alder. From the parking lot, a mowed path climbs a slope and winds over the tops of two hills: Mt. Baldy and Baskett Butte. (Flatlanders have the habit of giving names to any hump on the horizon.)

Two hundred yards or so into the hike, the trail forks. Although these forks later connect, the one you choose now determines what you'll find first. (You'll also come across a connecting path of about four miles that leads to Morgan Lake, but to protect both wintering and nesting birds, this loop trail is open only from May 1 till September 30.)

The right fork follows a curved, grassy path that skirts the slope of Baskett Butte and leads to an oak forest. Along this route in winter you'll scuff through leaves, pass beneath arching oaks, catch glimpses of deer and eagles, hear frogs and herons—and the wing beats and honks of geese. At the base of the oaks you can even find occasional owl droppings and pods, complete with mouse skeletons.

The left fork leads to the top of Mt. Baldy and a view of two major ponds—South Slough and Cottonwood, which are resting places during the day for ducks, geese, and herons—and the eagles and hawks that want to eat them. Beyond these ponds, stretching toward the mountain silhouettes rimming the valley, are grassy slopes, shrubby draws, oak-topped hills, old apple orchards, and flooded fields spotted with the splash of mallards and pintails.

Because for 22,000 dusky geese this is the land that greets them each fall and that holds them until spring when they begin their journey back to Alaska. A common sunrise spectacle in winter is a red-streaked eastern sky filled with ragged skeins of flapping wings and throaty honks. Hundreds, thousands of wings breathing through the morning air, whispering past.

Although the dusky is a Canada goose (please, don't call them Canadian), not all Canadas are the same, for 11 different subspecies come in three basic sizes—small, medium, and large. The largest (the giant Canada) can reach a weight of 18 pounds and a length of four feet, while the smallest (the cackling Canada) can be as small as two pounds and two feet. The dusky is somewhere in-between, weighing in at eight or nine pounds and stretching out to almost 30 inches. These differences, however, are limited only to the physical characteristics of Canada geese, for their personal traits seem universal.

Francis H. Kortright, whose work with waterfowl has set the standard for more than 50 years, describes the geese this way: "Sagacity, wariness, strength, and fidelity are characteristics of the Canada goose, which, collectively, are possessed in the same degree by no other bird. The Canada in many respects may serve as a model for man." These model traits include an almost unbreakable family unit, for these geese mate for life and share the work of raising their young. In the spring, the couple sets up housekeeping, staking out a territory of about 20 square feet that has both a clear view for protection and nearby water for the goslings. (To meet these requirements, it's not unusual for geese to nest in trees.) While the female nests, the male guards his mate with ferocious courage.

John James Audubon once tried to approach a nest and was attacked by the gander. "So daring was this fine fellow," Audubon wrote, "that in two instances he struck me a blow with his wings on the right arm which for an instant I thought was broken."

Through the summer, both parents raise the goslings, leading them on practice flights, conditioning them for fall's trip south. And when it's time to go, they leave as a family, joining other families at staging areas until flocks are formed, and the long journey begins. Frequently, this means getting junior past a gauntlet of hunters (three out of four geese killed are juveniles), and their courage and loyalty in doing this are responsible for an impressive collection of stories.

As an example, ornithologist E.W. Nelson described what he thought was a typical situation: "When one bird from a flock is shot, a single bird will often be seen to leave its companions at once and come circling about uttering loud calls. If the fallen bird is only wounded, its mate will invariably join it and may even allow itself to be approached and shot without attempting to escape."

The geese help one another in other ways as well. At the refuge, watch a skein in long flight or high wind, and you'll see individuals tradeoff on the tiring front position; watch a flock grazing in a field, and you'll see sentries standing alert while the others eat. Listen to mates greet each other, flocks hail each other, and sentinels cry out the approach of danger. If you watch and listen long enough, you might understand why some Indian tribes considered them to be powerful beings possessing great wisdom.

And the best time for visiting the geese is before they ride the wind back to the far north, flying back to a land where summer is becoming one long day, there to nest, to raise their families, and to wait for their winter return to an Oregon valley that has always been their home.

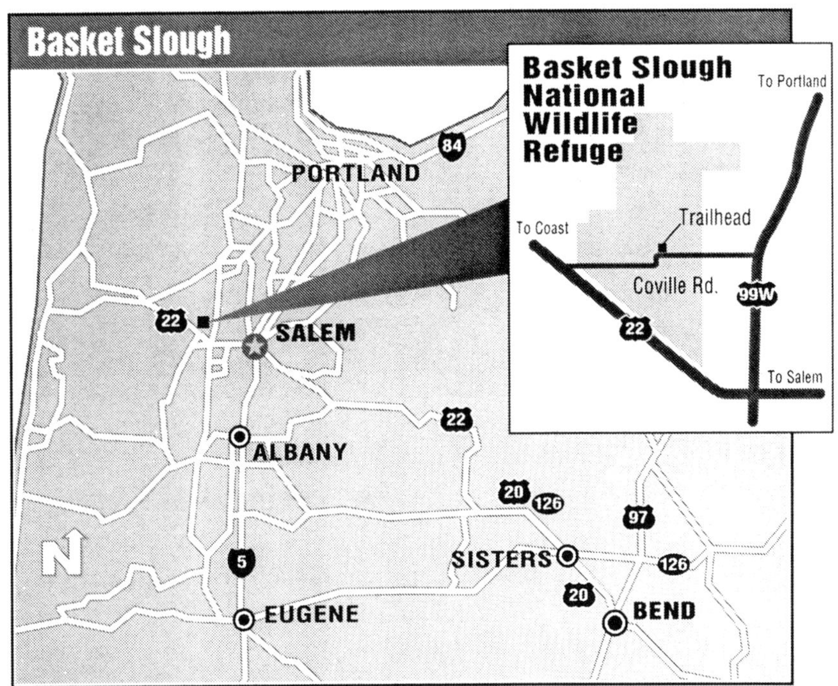

Where to Go

•The refuge is located near Highway 22 approximately 11 miles west of Salem.

What to Expect

•Roads and trails are open from sunrise to sunset, though some trails are closed during the winter to protect waterfowl.

•Keep your dog in the car. Please. Fido can make it tough on the birds. (Besides, if he gets into it with a dusky, better bet on the goose.)

Who to Contact

•For more information, call the refuge office at 541-757-7236.

Bob Straub Park

Tucked away on a spit of sand jutting from the Oregon coast is a park that sees more seals than people, hears more gull squawks than human voices. Even footprints are hard to find.

Bob Straub State Park, located on the north-central Oregon coast, is 483 acres of sand dunes, beach grass, and shore pines covering the spit that separates Nestucca Bay from the Pacific Ocean. "It's wonderful," says former Oregon governor Bob Straub, for whom the park is named. "So unchanged, such a prized section of beach."

A five mile hike will show you this prize, taking you on a loop along both sea shore and river bank. To find the park, drive toward Pacific City, and when you come into the wet, green valley of the Little Nestucca, where Holstein cows graze in the pastures and Haystack Rock looms in the distance, start looking for signs pointing the way.

Once you enter town, turn west on Sunset Drive and continue on to the parking lot at the end of the road. Here's you'll find rest rooms, picnic tables, running water, and beach access—but no trailhead. That's because the park contains no developed trails other than those punched through by horses and their riders. Even so, you'll find this a relatively easy hike, especially at low tide, when the packed sand gives better footing. So climb the dune line, hit the beach, and head south.

If your stroll meanders with the shoreline, it will pull you near the curl and splash of waves, toward the things gritty and kelpish and winged that live on the border between sea and land. "Look at that," says a woman along the beach with her Labrador retriever. She's searching for sand dollars and throwing sticks for her dog. "It's always the same, but it's always changing," she says, tipping her head toward the white-capped breakers rolling across a gray tide. "All this motion. It's beautiful."

Some park visitors, however, find one motion more disappointing than beautiful—the lurch of cars along the beach. Even though dune buggies and ATVs are restricted from this section of the coast, street-legal automobiles are permitted. This could be a holdover from the days when the Oregon coast was a state highway, and you might still encounter a driver who treats the beach as though it were paved. But for the most part, you have a good chance of having the place to yourself.

This relative seclusion, however, once almost proved to be the park's undoing when it joined a list of 66 state parks scheduled to be closed because of budget problems. "I can understand why people would put a low priority on it because very few people use the park, which is good," Straub says. "You can always be by yourself hiking up and down the beach."

The hike around the spit reaches the midway point when you reach the mouth of Nestucca Bay, where a driftwood forest lies on its back in the black sand, and the air smells like cold clam chowder. Sand spits like this one grow from wave action that cause "longshore drift," which occurs when waves break at an angle to the shoreline. This forces the current to flow parallel to the land, pushing sand along the beach and building spits across the mouths of rivers and bays.

At the far end of Bob Straub Park, this natural funnel attracts seals, which gather to hunt the salmon that enter the bay on their upstream spawning trips into both the Nestucca and the Little Nestucca Rivers. When the seals spot visitors, they slide into the water, float and snort past, then wriggle back onto the beach for a nap.

To see another side of the park, stay on the river side of the spit, where dunes give way to lines of firs and spruce. From here

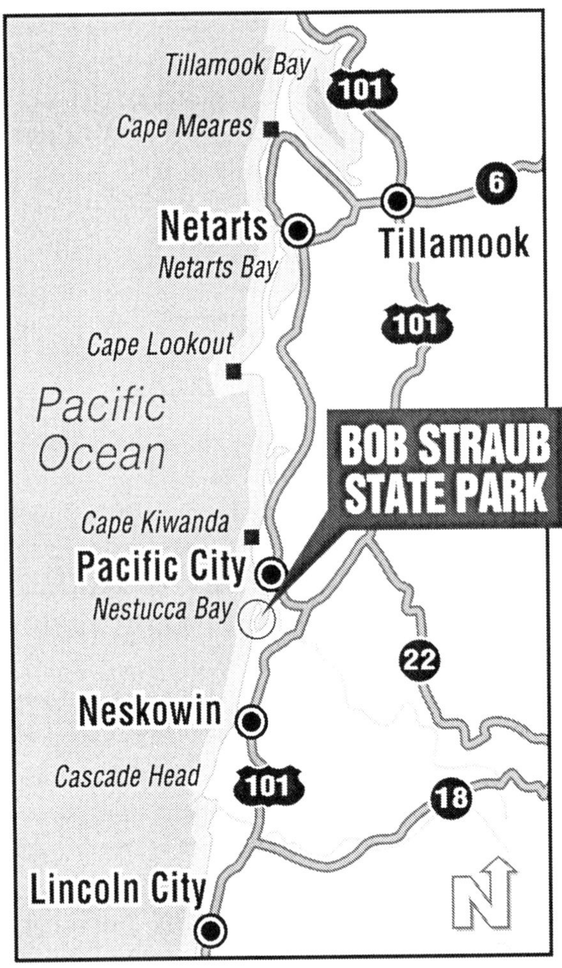

you can follow either the river or a trail back to where you began. The trail slices through the high bank, just before the first bend in the river, and right where the fir trees ends.

"But you gotta be looking for it," says a hiker familiar with the park. "The river route is longer, but the inland trail is brushier. Take your pick."

The trail takes you from beach and tidewater to forest and wetlands. The brush is soft and wet, and the smells of a mud flat-tide, seaweed, and salt—follow you through it. A Jungle Jim machete would be handy in places where slugs dangle from the huckleberries and skeeters whine through the salal, but the extra work takes you into an area where deer wander nearby and ducks fly overhead.

When you reach a crossroads with an intersecting path, either go straight to the service road that leads back to the parking lot, or turn right to continue on to the paved boat launch on the bank of the Nestucca River. On the other hand, you might decide to postpone your return by taking the left fork, which leads back onto the spit, a sanctuary of sand and trees, where the next strong wind will blow away your footprints.

Where to Go

•Pacific City is located off Highway 101, approximately 25 miles north of Lincoln City.

When to Go

•The park is open for day-use only.

What to Expect

•Fishing season for Chinook salmon can mean heavy use of the Nestucca River and its bay.

Things to Know

•No English translation exists for the Indian word Nestucca.

•Robert Straub served as state senator from 1959-1963, as state treasurer from 1964-1972, and as governor from 1975-1979.

Who to Contact

•For more information, call the State Parks District Office at 503-842-3182.

Cape Lookout

For millions of years the Pacific Ocean has been doing its best to pound Oregon's Cape Lookout into the sea. But the cape hangs on. Jutting two miles into the ocean and rising 800 feet above it, the headland stands as part of Cape Lookout State Park, over 2,000 acres of campgrounds and coastline—and one trail that leads to the tip of the cape, where you can see what happens when a chunk of basalt takes arms against a sea of trouble.

The cape is a remnant of a volcanic island that formed when the Columbia River gathered up Eastern Oregon's lava and poured it out onto the northern Oregon coast 15 million years ago. But then the lava cooled, the rain fell, and the basalt began collecting soil and sprouting trees. Now the five mile round trip takes you through a rain forest of hemlock and spruce, whose moss-covered trunks seem as thick as whales.

The journey begins at the trailhead's parking lot, which you'll find along the Three Capes Scenic Loop, a spur off Highway 101. The trailhead sign is confusing because it offers you three trails, but you'll only see two—one heading north to the park's campground, and one heading south to the end of the cape. Step behind the sign and take the left-hand trail.

Before long—maybe a couple hundred yards—you'll come to a fork. Keep straight ahead; the left fork is that missing third trail, a continuation of the Oregon Coast Trail, which leads two miles down to the beach. The path you've taken will give you a gradual 400-foot drop to the end of the cape with only a few switchbacks over a rain-spattered trail, and plank walkways cover the worst of the muddy hollows.

In this land that soaks up over 100 inches of rain per year, the air is often mist—soft and hazy, but still thrumming with the sounds of surf rolling against the rocks and wrens singing you down the trail. On a clear day, the cape's southern edge, which holds the trail along an almost vertical slope plunging to the sea, gives you glimpses of the beach far below.

Other views on blue-sky days can include such famous Oregon landmarks as Haystack Rock, Cascade Head, Cape Meares, and Neahkahnie Mountain. But even if you're caught in coastal mist, the forest by itself is reason enough to take this walk, for as the trail meanders along, it takes you through a tunnel of green. Overhead, storm-beaten spruce lean down to escape the wind; root wads spread wide like a roof, and the shattered and toppled trunks of snags make sky bridges.

Just before reaching the tip of the cape, you emerge from this tunnel onto the edge of a wind-scoured slope. At the end, you'll find a cliff-top meadow where dandelions, yarrow, and roses cling to the

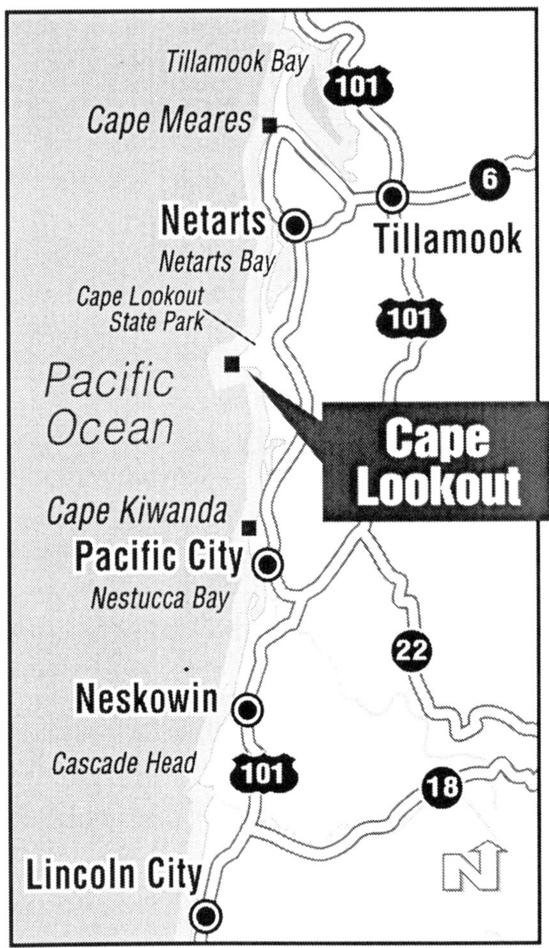

edges, and where squat spruce trees grow out instead of up so they can duck the wind.

Along this rock ledge people sit, whispering to one another as though in church, gazing down at the flight of gulls and the rolling swirl of mist and sea, of white and gray. On the water a dory circles. A buoy moans. And everywhere is the glide and swoop of birds; more than 150 species have been recorded here, and the white-splattered rocks show it.

"Is that a whale?" someone whispers, then points. The ledge-sitters lean forward and peer toward a whirling circle of sea that slackens, then rolls beneath a wave. Even though no tail flashes, no back rolls, it's enough to make you catch your breath, wait, and let your eyes turn the shine of salt water into the glisten of whale skin.

But maybe next time it will be a whale, for the tip of the cape is known as a primary whale watching site. Some experts say that between December and June, as many as 20,000 California gray whales migrate through these waters on their trip between Alaska and Mexico, and that as many as 30 per hour will slide past this headland's point.

The gray whales begin this migration in mid to late fall, when they leave their summer home in the Bering Sea and heads south for their wintering grounds near the Baja Peninsula. There they find both winter shelter and willing mates, and when they begin their spring trip north, they're accompanied by their ton-and-a-half calves.

Thanks to a half century of protection from whaling, which has brought the whales back from an 1898 population of 2,000 and 1940s numbers that almost pushed them into the abyss of extinction, these calves will make the same trip next year without worrying about dodging harpoons.

Although south-in-winter, north-in-spring is the normal pattern of the 12,000 mile round trip migration, you don't have to wait for that schedule to go whale watching; an estimated 400-500 gray whales have decided they like the Oregon coast so much that it has become their summer home.

So no matter what the season, out on the tip of this ancient volcanic island, the sea keeps pounding, the whales keep swimming, and the cape offers you a seat where you can watch it all happen.

When to Go

•During the last week of December and the week of college spring vacation, volunteers at Cape Lookout help you spot whales.

Where to Go

•The trailhead parking lot is located 14 miles south of Tillamook on the Three Capes Scenic Loop.

What to Expect

•Bikes and horses are prohibited on the trail.

Things to Know

•In 1788, British explorer John Meares gave the name Cape Lookout to the cape lying ten miles to the north. That name was later changed to Cape Meares.

•In 1935, the U.S. Lighthouse Service donated the land for the park.

Who to Contact

•For information about the park, call 503-842-4981.

•For information about whale watching, call 541-563-2002.

Finley Refuge

If the land holds memories, then Oregon remembers a west-side valley where prairie grass bristled beneath the bellies of elk and fluttered with the wing beats of geese. And when the first settlers arrived in this valley of the Willamette River, one of the most important parts of their new found world was this grass—more than a million acres of it.

"The grass here is a great portion of the wealth of the country," wrote an 1850s settler, "and without it we would be as hard up as the people of Ireland without potatoes."

Even so, valley settlers went to work plowing the prairie into pastures and planting the grassland to crops. For more than a century they toiled, and when the last of the prairie was almost gone, so were the geese. Perhaps only the valley's refuges, established in the 1960s, saved them. Chief among these is the William L. Finley National Wildlife Refuge, which is distinguished by both its habitat and its history.

With over 5,000 acres—more than eight square miles—Finley has enough room for crops and hedges, forests and hills, marshes and ponds. Its habitat is managed to preserve the area's historic environment of woodlands, wetlands, and grasslands, including the valley's largest remaining tract of native prairie. (Of the valley's one million acres of prairie grass, only about a thousand acres remain.)

"If you can shut out the sound of an occasional airplane or chain saw," says a recent visitor to the refuge, "you can almost make yourself believe you've stepped back a thousand years."

The best way to experience this for yourself is to hike the patrol road that starts at headquarters and loops through the heart of the refuge. At nearby Cabell Marsh, willows and maples form a tangled wall on the far edges of a meadow, and geese swim on the water near brushy islands of native grass and wild roses. In the shallows, catfish lurk, frogs squeak—and more geese strut out onto the bank and start down the road. "Watch out for the goose poop," says a woman on the trail.

Along the edges of the two-track path, raccoon tracks dent the mud, lupine petals spot the fields, and moss tendrils sway in the oaks. From out of the ash—thick, puddled backwaters rise the whistles of wood ducks. Other trails lead from this road to Muddy Creek, Cattail Pond, Pigeon Butte, or Beaver Pond. These detours might take you to where elk drink from the ponds, wrens build their nests, or beavers chew the ash trees.

It's the prairie grass, however, that sets this place apart. When the stir of wind is the only sound, the bend of grass the only movement, your imagination almost sees through the centuries, back to the small villages and narrow footpaths leading through the forests and meadows—for this was once the land of the Kalapuya, the valley's native people. And the open, grassy prairies that once thrived here were the work not of nature, but of the Kalapuya.

No one knows how long these people had lived in the valley by the time the first settlers arrived, but we do know that theirs was a land of water shaped by fire. "It was the custom of these Indians, late in the autumn...to burn off the whole country," wrote Jesse Applegate, whose family converted a Hudson Bay Company pack trail into the Applegate Trail, the valley's major wagon route that once passed through this area.

The effect of these fires was to kill brush and seedlings, keeping open both the valley floor and its hillsides. The reason for the fires was food. After old grass burned, new grass sprouted, and the Kalapuya hunted the deer and elk that came to graze it; fire also kept open the meadows necessary for growing camas and tarweed, two staples of their diet.

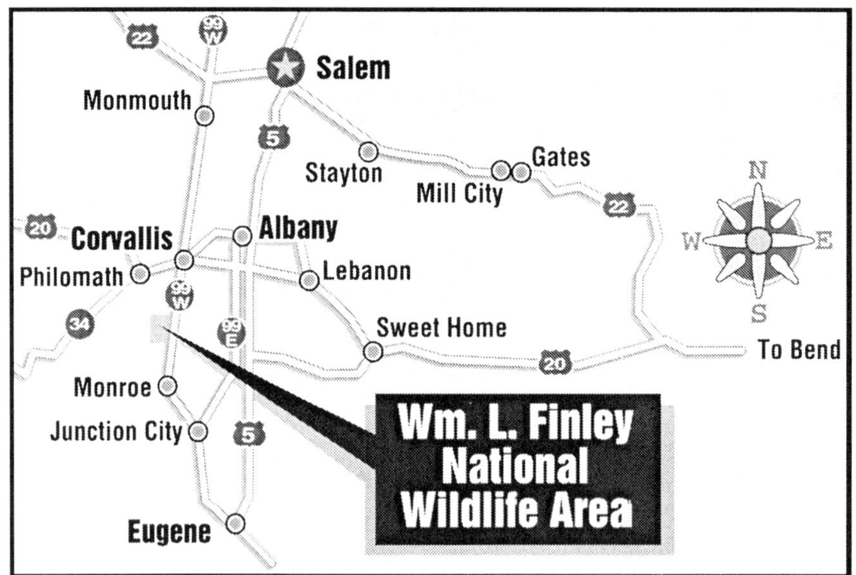

In this way, the Kalapuya turned the land from dense forest to open prairie and savanna, spotted with scattered patches of native oaks—California black and Oregon white—that survived the grass fires because of their thick bark."Some of the early settlers thought the oak groves were orchards," says Finley's Greg Hughes, who wants to reintroduce fire as a major management tool.

But when these settlers entered the land of the Kalapuya, they found few of its people, for most of them were dead before the first covered wagons entered the Oregon Country. The reason was an epidemic of malaria—sometimes called Rocky Mountain Fever—that struck in the early 1830s. By the time it ended, more than three out of four Kalapuya lay dead.

"These [Kalapuya] children came to us almost naked, in a very filthy state, and covered with vermin," wrote Cyrus Sheard, a mission teacher, in 1835.

So pioneer cabins replaced Kalapuya villages, but the untilled land reverted back to forests and thickets. To help maintain the land as it was in pre-homestead days, the refuge today uses a combination of farming and grazing. Even though the main purpose of this effort is to provide wintering grounds for dusky Canada geese, which winter only in the Willamette Valley, the refuge also wants to "provide protection and habitat for wildlife species other than waterfowl."

As a result, Finley residents include deer and bear, grouse and pheasant, bald eagles and peregrine falcons—even elk, for a small herd now makes its home on the refuge. To see this environment, take a walk along the Woodpecker Loop and the adjoining Mill Hill trail, which take you through a range of refuge habitat.

Beginning near the refuge's western border, the loop leads over a stream, through a forest, and onto a slope that wanders past meadows, savannas, swales, and a pond. A junction then sends you down the "Inter-Tie Trail," which connects to Mill Hill. After cutting

Where to Go

- The main refuge entrance is near milepost 93 on Highway 99W, located 11 miles south of Corvallis.

When to Go

- Refuge roads and trails are open from sunrise to sunset, though some areas are open to the public only from May 1 until October 31.
- Woodpecker Loop and Mill Hill are open year-round.
- Winter is the best time to see geese and raptors; spring, to see songbirds and shorebirds.

What to Expect

- Dogs and bikes are prohibited from trails.
- If you get off the pathways, you're almost guaranteed to run into poison oak.

Things to Know

- The Kalapuya were divided into as many as 20 bands that spoke three different dialects of the same language. The refuge site was the home of the Chemmapho, or Muddy Creek, band.
- The refuge is named for William L. Finley, who helped persuade Theodore Roosevelt to establish the first national wildlife refuges in the West.
- Evidence from tree rings indicates that a 1690 fire burned a half million acres of the Willamette Valley.

Who to Contact

- For more information about the refuge, call the refuge office at 541-757-7236.

through a forest of oaks and firs, the path turns onto a gravel road where quail can flush from the edges, and then passes a red barn, the home of a great horned owl.

The Mill Hill trail is like a park without the mowed lawns and tossed Frisbees. You'll find spots of sun and scents of soil, flowered fields and sitting benches, grassy clearings and marshy edges before wandering back to the Woodpecker Loop.

Near the end of the walk is an example of what can happen to an untended Willamette Valley, for the refuge was a farm for more than a century, and here a wrecked gate and a sagging fence border an abandoned pasture. When the cattle stopped grazing it, brambles and thickets took over. Nearby, only a few old oaks and maples are left standing, yet thousands of saplings sprout from the ground. It's a clear lesson of what would happen if the land were left alone.

"I have seen millions of acres of breeding grounds pass under the drain and the plow," Emerson Hough wrote in 1912, "so that the passing whisper of the wild fowl's wing has been forgotten there now for many years."

But today those whispering wings have returned, for this part of the Willamette Valley remembers not only the Kalapuya who burned it and the settlers who plowed it, but also the refuge that saved it.

The Road to Idiotville

The sound of the town's name lured me like a Sirens' song—Idiotville. Yet it was more than the word on a map, for the ghostly box marking its site and the red squiggle tracing its road beckoned to me, whispered to me that here I might find family roots, kindred spirits. The idea, of course, was absurd; only a fool—or an idiot—would follow such a reckless adventure. So I packed the car and set out on the road to Idiotville.

Oregon Highway 6. That's what they call the road now. Its confluence with Highway 26 west of Portland is called Tillamook Junction, 24 miles from Portland (population more than 500,000), 52 miles to Tillamook (population less than 5,000). And somewhere in-between lay Idiotville, situated on the western edge of the Coast Range summit.

From the junction, the asphalt stretches into a land of fields and farms, past fir forests and oak bottoms framed with green and mist, and housing developments that all seem to be painted beige. When the road enters a corridor of trees, a gloam of fir boughs hang overhead, forming a shadowy tunnel where stores and restaurants sell gas, groceries, tackle, and bait—the mainstays of the steelheaders that swarm here to fish the Wilson River. And because I've fished for steelhead before, have stood hip deep in roiling water while ice glazed against me, I could sense Idiotville not far away.

In fact, its history was at that moment rolling beneath my tires because for more than 100 years this river road has been the main link between the Tillamook and Willamette Valleys, crossing a land almost unknown by early coast and valley settlers, who kept their distance from the steep slopes, the wet brush, and the tangled forests.

So rugged is this part of the Coast Range that the first whites to cross did it by accident. It happened in 1867, when two elk hunters from the Willamette Valley side of the mountains became lost and wandered into the Wilson River canyon. Six days later, the last three days spent eating only snails, they stumbled out of the brush at Tillamook.

Even though folks on the coast were almost desperate for a road to the outside, they didn't try the hunters' route again for another eight years. The results were almost the same. When they began building the road in 1875, the survey party got lost and nearly starved. After that, they left the Wilson River canyon alone for quite a spell.

But in the late 1880s, homesteaders began slashing their way into the Wilson River country, staking their claims, building their cabins, and setting up house. Some of the first of those homesteaders settled near what the map shows as the site of Idiotville, some two dozen or so miles uphill from Tillamook, near the headwaters of the river.

These people lived in a time of wattle chimneys and dirt floors, of puncheon furniture and snowbound winters; packhorses hauled the supplies and wolves roamed the woods. When times got better, there were flour sacks for curtains, beef tallow for candles, and kerosene for lanterns.

In the 1890s, however, big changes came to the canyon country—first a telegraph, then a toll road and a stage line. As one descendent of pioneers remembers it, "the country opened to the flux of travelers and campers that turned the wilderness into a well traveled road."

Knowing that the pioneer spirit probably still flowed in the veins of those Idiotville folks, I wondered about the family roots and kindred spirits I was sure to find there. Would they be like me, thick-bellied and balding, unable to carry a tune? Or would they be whipcord lean, rawhide tough, as bone rugged as the basalt of the Wilson River's canyon, their eyes dark as its firs—and as fiery, for the loggers who followed the homesteaders saw the forests aflame and the canyon scorched. And as the road climbs more steeply along alder laced creek bottoms and toward a summit high enough to hold snow even in spring, it enters the land those people knew as the Tillamook Burn.

Here in the 18 years between 1933 and 1951, four fires burned more than 500 square miles of Coast Range forests. It is said that the heat cracked cliffs and the ash fell so heavily on Tillamook that it had to be shoveled from the streets. Today, however, the land has healed, and the summit is a doorway to what *The Oregonian* says is some of "the most developed recreation areas in the northern Coast Range."

Indeed, the signs marking the entrances to the Tillamook State Forest's campgrounds and trailheads whooshed past, but there was no sign for Idiotville, and the road was tipping toward the sea. Where oh where was Idiotville? Where were the family roots and kindred spirits? The map showed that it lay between the campground at Gales Creek and the trailhead for Kings Mountain.

But then those places, too, whooshed past, and the road tipped some more on its way down the western ramp of the mountain, winding with the river now, streams of water plunging off the slopes and spilling off rock in a gush and a splash that showed why this has long been a road to disaster. For this land has a history not only of lost people and forest fires, but also of mud slides. In 1963 and again in 1991, parts of the mountain tumbled across the road, burying the main artery between coast and valley. Could Idiotville have ridden away with the topple and plunge of rock and mud?

I clenched myself tight against such a thought, and by the time I reached Lee's Camp, a store and gas pump, it was clear that I'd missed Idiotville, failed to see the turnoff. Went right past it, probably. Made me feel like such a...well, such an idiot. This, of course, made me even more determined to find it, so I kept heading toward Tillamook, looking for someone who could show me the way.

From here the land flattens and the river broadens and the signs along the road tell you that the forests here were planted in the 1950s, about the time the last Tillamook Burn blazed itself out. Green and slack the river flows, with occasional basalt boulders that curl the water white. Down the road, shuttle services and RV parks flash their signs near the bright green pastures of dairy farms. Here and there along this stretch, elk stand along the roadside, some of them grazing on the edge of clearcuts, others staring at traffic, as though waiting to cross.

Perhaps it was desperation that made me pull up alongside one of those elk, perhaps the light of intelligence glinting from her eyes. Or maybe, just maybe, it was another whisper from another Siren. The reason is unimportant. The way I figure it, you go looking for Idiotville, you don't have to follow any rules. So I stopped the car and rolled down the window.

"Excuse me," I said. The elk glanced back over her shoulder, as though expecting company. "Excuse me—but could you tell me how to find Idiotville?" But then the slow blink of her dark eyes told me she thought I had already found it.

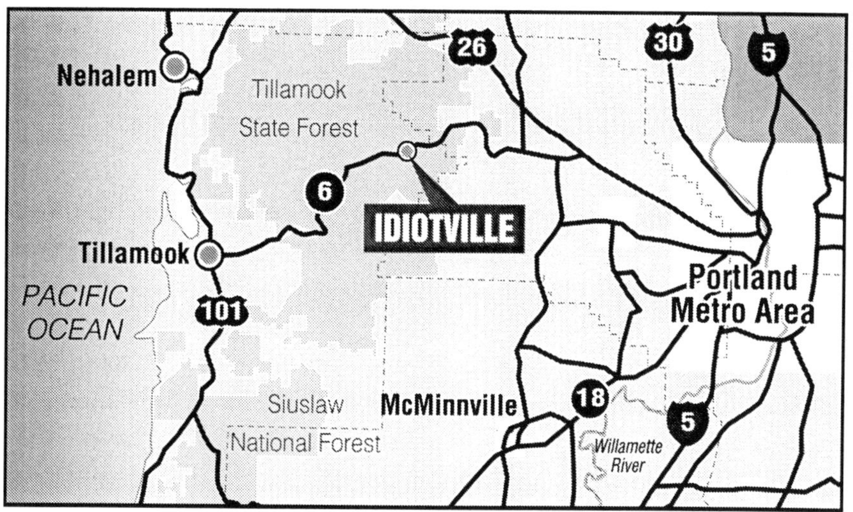

Where to Go

• Tillamook Junction, the eastern end of Highway 6, is approximately 24 miles northwest of Portland on Highway 26 (the road that goes past the zoo).

When to Go

• Try to avoid weekends. That's when Portland spills over onto the coast roads.

What to Expect

• You won't find Idiotville on most maps; in fact, you might find it on only one—the Oregon map created by Imus Geographics in Eugene.

Things to Know

• The Wilson River was first called the Georgie River. Local settlers renamed it to honor the man who started Tillamook's dairy industry by driving the first herd of cows from Seaside to Tillamook in 1851.

• The first river road was completed in 1893.

Who to Contact

• Sorry—Idiotville apparently has nobody to contact.

Leach Botanical Garden

In his 90 years of living, John Leach faced one of his biggest challenges while courting a botanist named Lilla Irvin. "She never said NO to me," Leach wrote. "She said PHOOEY." Then one day he found the way to her heart.

"When I told Lilla I could tie the diamond hitch, talk mule talk, reason with mule logic, and take her into the wildest country, where no cake-eating botanists could get, she fell on my neck so hard that I never recovered." So after their 1913 wedding, John and Lilla spent the next 59 years sharing the adventure of their lives together, exploring some of Oregon's most remote areas in a quest for plants.

And when it was over, the Leaches left behind a legacy of not only scientific discoveries and collections, but also a home that became Portland's first public botanical garden. Since it opened to the public in 1983, the garden has shown thousands of visitors the results of the Leaches' passion for plants.

"The purpose of the Leach Botanical Garden is much like that of a museum," says Jessica Sall, the curator who describes herself as a plant nerd formerly of Nebraska. "We preserve specimens as well as provide research, education, and enjoyment." Through the nine acre site bordering Johnson Creek in southeast Portland, a network of trails shows you how some of this comes together.

Before beginning the tour, however, you should know that this place also preserves the memory of the two extraordinary people who created it. As one of the garden's newsletters points out, a visit here is incomplete "without any knowledge of John and Lilla, their adventures, collections, or how the garden was created." So don't be alarmed at the spirits you find here; they're friendly.

One trail climbs the north slope above the house. Here rock-lined paths wind through groves of trees, layers of shrubs, and beds of flowers. Even the Willamette Valley winter can't stop the growing. As a woman along the trail says, "This time of year, the garden is a good place to come for anyone with cabin fever, anyone who just has to see a flower or a bud."

Starting in 1931, the Leaches laid the foundation for this landscaping, building a mile of trails as well as planting a thousand species of trees and hundreds of plants. This has given the garden what Sall calls a "strong and mature collection."

Near the top of the hill lies a nursery, which holds a collection of seeds from around the world. "We not only grow the plants we use in the garden," Sall says, "but the ones we sell at the plant sales."

These sales are part of the fundraising activities carried out by the Leach Garden Friends, a group of volunteers that gives as many as 12,000 hours every year to jobs such as raising money, growing plants, and maintaining buildings and grounds. It seems to be a labor of love that springs from a devotion to the Leaches as well as to the garden. As Sall says, "We're all dedicated to what the Leaches started."

Such dedication has helped the garden grow from its original five acres to its present nine, an expansion that leaves room for future projects that will emphasize collections native to the Northwest, including a medicinal herb garden, a Willamette Valley grassland, a mountain moraine, and a conifer collection. "Our gardening philosophy is to build a timeless garden," Sall says, "one that always works, one that isn't a reaction to gardening trends or fads."

The garden's appearance reflects this philosophy, for it is maintained through extensive rather than intensive management, which means the plants live their natural cycles without excessive snipping, lopping, and other fussing. "A garden is always changing," Sall says, "so we try to display plants in a natural context rather than in a perfectly groomed landscape."

This attitude seems to echo the Leaches' passion for the untamed side of life. "The whole world was ours to do with as we

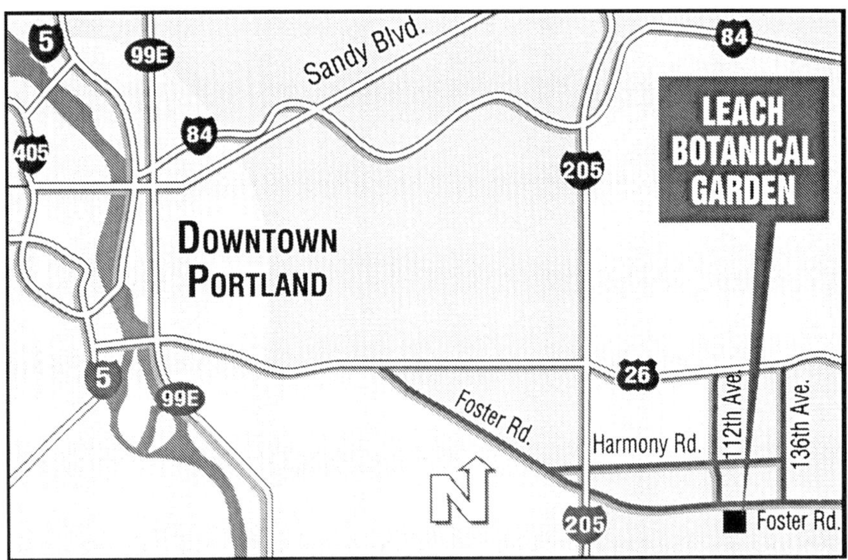

pleased," John wrote in 1966, a half dozen years before his death. "We loved to explore new country and find new plants." With only two pack burros for company, the Leaches wore out numerous pairs of hiking boots on their botanical wanderings through roadless, relatively unexplored land. John, a pharmacist by trade, handled the packing while Lilla scouted for plants.

"Together we climbed the lovely, lonely, unmapped ridges and glades of the wildest parts of our West," John wrote, "from the Rocky Mountains to the Pacific coast, sometimes going in over snow in the spring and sometimes being driven out by it in the fall."

Their frequent journeys into the Western wilds resulted in Lilla's discovery of five plants new to science. Among these, perhaps the most important was her 1930 finding of Kalmiopsis leachiana.

"Suddenly, we came upon a breathtaking sight," she said later about her discovery. "Before us, beside the trail, lay a patch of low evergreen bushlets, simply covered with deep rose flowers, vividly pink in the sunshine. Thrilled? We were! I felt sure I had found something new." It was new, all right—and important. Lilla's discovery led to the establishment of two botanical areas as well as the Kalmiopsis Wilderness Area in the Siskiyou Mountains of southwest Oregon's Curry County.

Because this corner of Oregon was one of the Leaches' favorites, a second garden trail leads down a flight of stone steps to the creek, where a special area grows plants native to the Siskiyous. Nestled beneath the conifer canopy is a stone cabin that the Leaches used as a summer home and weekend retreat while carpenters built the main house, which was finished in 1936.

Inside that house today, time still seems to be treading through the 1930s—the arched beams and the paneled walls, the calm of the garden and the view of the grounds. The sense that here lived people who loved their home, their work, and their life together.

It was a home, John said, that "held our attention, love, affection and the greatest effort of our lives for 35 years." And today, the door to that home is still open to those who find their way to the Leaches' garden.

Where to Go

•The garden is located near the corner of Portland's Foster Road and 122nd Avenue. (From Interstate 205, take Exit 17.)

When to Go

•The garden is open Tuesday through Saturday from 9 am until 4 pm, and Sunday from 1 pm until 4 pm. It is closed Mondays and major holidays.

•Depending on the season, garden tours are available on either Saturdays or Wednesdays through most of the year.

What to Expect

•Approximately 20,000-30,000 people visit the garden each year, with peak times coming in February and March.

Things to Know

•John Leach, who was raised in Morrow County, lived from 1882 until 1972; Lilla, from the northern Willamette Valley, lived from 1886-1980.

•The Leaches made over 6,000 plant collections.

•The garden's horticultural library is said to hold the largest collection north of San Francisco.

•The Leaches' ashes were scattered in the Kalmiopsis Wilderness in 1992.

Who to Contact

•For more information about either the garden or the Friends, call 503-761-9503.

Minto-Brown Island

John Minto fell in love with Oregon on what you might call a blind date. "In a school geography," he wrote, "I saw...a half page description of Oregon...that page was thumbed until it was very dark. I would take it up as I came out of the coal mine, and look at that old book."

So in 1844, 22-year-old John Minto, a native Englishman transplanted to the Pennsylvania coal mines, went looking for a home at the end of the Oregon Trail. He found it in Salem—Oregon's capital city on the bank of the Willamette River. Here Minto's accomplishments as a farmer, surveyor, writer, and legislator eventually put his name on the wall of the state Capitol as one of "158 men and women who helped shape Oregon's history."

More important than his name, however, is the land he left behind. Located approximately two miles from downtown Salem, it is now part of Minto-Brown Island, an 883 acre park that serves as a wildlife refuge, a recreation area, and a vital link between Salem's past and its future.

This park, says the city, is a special place that blends "farming, recreation, and wildlife in an urban environment." This means that here you have the chance to wander for miles beneath trees, along water, and through fields.

"What I like most about it," says a woman who visits the park often, "is its variety. You can fly a kite, walk your dog, or ride your bicycle there. You can even fish or canoe if you want—and it's so close to town."

The park began as two separate islands. Near the Willamette's west bank lay the island—home of Isaac "Whiskey" Brown, a former Astorian who settled here in 1857 and began raising livestock and tobacco. Near its east bank was the island belonging to John Minto, who came along ten years after Brown. After clearing the land, Minto farmed it, specializing in raising sheep. Through the years, however, the flooding Willamette River changed its channel, and the islands merged.

Today, Minto-Brown Island is an area of sloughs and backwaters, of old river channels and thick underbrush, of grassy meadows and crowded cottonwoods, of bridges arching over slackwater and fields lying both fallow and tilled, with different parts of their almost 250 acres either planted for market or left for wildlife.

Through this mixed landscape weaves a web of trails that gives you the chance to bike or stroll through what is a home for 175 species of birds and 35 species of mammals—including deer, raccoons, foxes, beavers, and rabbits. Lots of rabbits. It also serves as a wintering ground for dusky Canada geese, which use it heavily from October till April.

Five miles of asphalt paths lead out from two main parking lots and connect into roughly a dozen loops of varying lengths, so you can pick the route that best fits your interests and endurance. As an example of one loop that gives you a sweep around much of the old Minto and Brown farms, head out of the first parking lot and follow the bike route sign to your left.

This route begins near a pond with banks grazed and tromped by white geese, whose flapping and paddling can stir the pond-lilied water brown. Past here, the pavement curves along the tree line and beneath sweeping branches as it carries you through the scent of grass and soil and mist.

Along the way you'll find that many walkers and runners say hello, a rare greeting in many cities. "It's a beautiful morning," says a woman jogger, whose Basset hound clumps along behind her.

After following near the river channel of John Minto's day, the trail first breaks out into fields of blackberry brambles, and then ends at nearby Homestead Road. Although this is not a designated

bike path, you can still follow it for a mile to reach a far corner of the park. Past fields and orchards stretches Homestead Road, then to a parking lot turnoff, where a trail leads down to a slough. If you take the side trip, you'll cut through a filbert orchard to find one of the park's many waterside platforms, which people use for both fishing and bird watching.

Down the road, the bike route picks up again at a road barricade from which hangs a "Street Closed" sign. (If you get to the turnoff for the Demolition Landfill, you've gone too far.) This barrier blocks the park's old access road, now closed to cars. Once you go around it and head down that road, you'll pass the old parking lot and park entrance sign.

On this distant edge of Minto-Brown Island are relative solitude and silence. In the distance is a thread of traffic noise, but mostly you'll hear birdy whistles and chirps. Remember the smells of camping when you were a kid? Water and trees and smoke? Somehow those smells are still here in the early morning. So are herons and pheasants, orioles and doves, and rabbits. Lots of rabbits.

When you come out into a tree-ringed field of grass and soil, you'll probably find geese grazing nearby. From here, the path bends past the geese, crosses a bridge, and heads toward the second parking lot and the beginning of a route that takes you first along the bank of the Willamette River, then past a patchwork of fields, and finally back to the starting point. When you reach the parking lot, you'll have just circled most of what was once the farmland of John Minto and Whiskey Brown.

These pioneers probably wouldn't recognize Salem today. From the approximately 1,000 people who lived here when Minto bought his island, the city grew to 17,000 by the time of his death in 1915, then to 70,000 by the time the city bought his land in 1970. Yet to many of the almost 120,000 people who now live in the capital city but who still need trees and water and space, Minto-Brown Island is more important than ever.

So John Minto, the man who by day worked in a Pennsylvania coal mine and by night read about the Oregon Country, finally found what he was looking for on an island in the Willamette River. And today it's still there for us to find.

Where to Go

• The park is located west of Salem's Commercial Street and along the bank of the Willamette River.

When to Go

• Minto-Brown Island is open daily from dawn till dusk.

Things to Know

• Salem, which was settled by the Methodist missionary Jason Lee in 1840, became the state capital (1851) before it became an incorporated city (1857).

• You'll find the name of John Minto (1822-1915) in the Capitol's House Chamber. In Salem he was known as "Uncle John."

Who to Contact

• For more information, contact the Salem Regional Parks and Recreation Agency at 503-588-6261, though you might not find anybody to talk to.

Peavy Arboretum

Because we live in a time that sometimes portrays loggers as villains, some of the guys with the chain saws are fighting back. But they're not cranking up their Stihls—they're growing trees; and they're not cutting down the woods—they're inviting you into them so you can see what can be the future of Oregon's forests.

One of the state's biggest welcome maps lies at the entrance to the Peavy Arboretum, located in the foothills of the Coast Range near Corvallis. Displayed on this 40 acre site are over 200 trees and shrubs collected from the Northwest as well as other parts of both the nation and the world.

Yet the arboretum is more than just an exhibit, for it serves as a hub from which a network of trails leads into the McDonald Research Forest, a 7,000 acre "laboratory for research and education" managed by Oregon State University's College of Forestry.

Realizing the importance of such a laboratory means understanding the size of Oregon's 30 million acres of woodlands, which make up almost half the state's land. So imagine a forest 16 miles wide that runs from the Pacific to the Atlantic; now let's say you're the one who has to take care of all those trees. What do you do? Well, the McDonald Forest is a place to learn what works and what doesn't, a place to study both the ecology and the management of a forest that is meant to last for all the generations to come.

To let you see how things are working so far, the forest's eight miles of hiking paths and over sixty miles of multiple-use trails and roads are open to travel by foot, bicycle, or horse. Trail guides, available at trailheads, list the different routes, which range from a half-mile stroll that begins and ends at a parking lot, to bike treks that take you across the mountain.

A good way to get acquainted with the area is to hike the Forest Discovery Trail, a mile-and-a-half path through trees and over streams that takes you to what has been called "a hodgepodge of tree species." The reason for the diversity is that Peavy Arboretum once served as the state's tree nursery, and because some foresters couldn't resist experimenting, they planted some seedlings in combinations that don't occur in the wild.

For example, a short uphill climb from the trailhead will take you to ponderosa pines (usually happier east of the Cascades) growing near Pacific madrones (more common to the coast). Then as you continue uphill—to a gravel road, which you cross before heading up again—you'll enter a Douglas fir plantation. Here you'll find the world's most valuable timber species growing in straight, spaced rows like a giant's cone orchard.

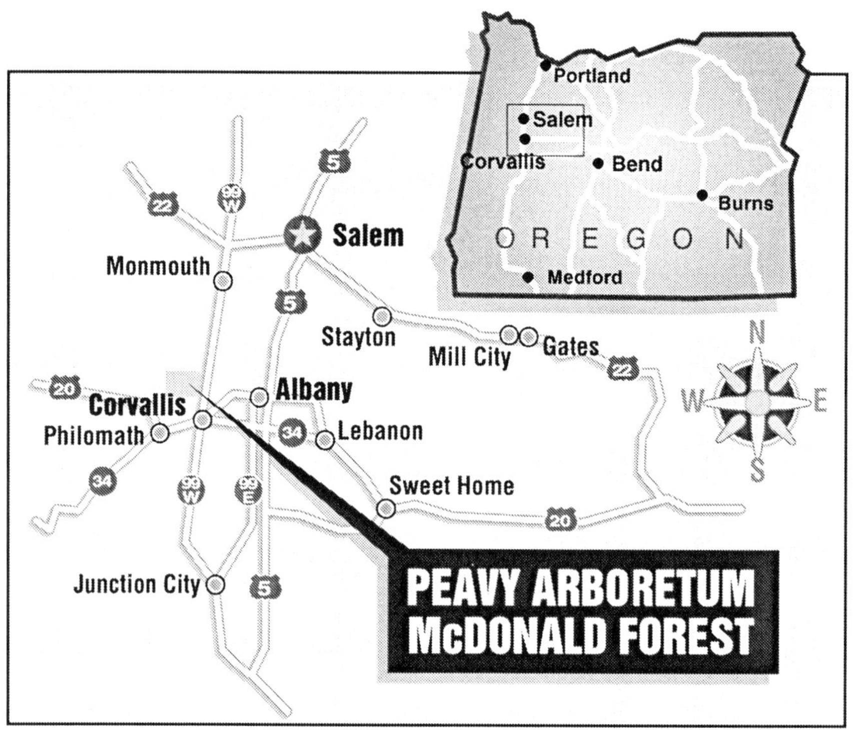

You might also find the rough-skinned newt, a brown-backed, orange-bellied salamander that resembles a Jurassic Park miniature. "Don't eat it," says a woman along the trail with her Labrador retriever. She looks a lot like my wife—the woman, not the Lab—so I listen to her out of habit. "Its skin carries a powerful toxin," she says, pointing to the newt. The man walking with her nods in agreement.

She goes on to tell the legend of a pioneer who goes down to a stream in the dark, scoops out a bucket of water containing a single rough-skinned newt, and then unknowingly boils it all up for coffee. The first cup of java kills him. A kind of Darwinism operating along the Oregon Trail. The story works; I refrain from eating the newt.

At the upper end of the Douglas fir patch, the slope first flattens into a bench, then thickens with an understory of smaller trees—hazel and dogwood, thimbleberry and cascara buckthorn. If you feel like playing Daniel Boone about now, you can use the hazel nuts for a snack, the dogwood bark to cure malaria, and the thimbleberry leaves for tissue. But don't use the cascara "for roasting hot dogs or marshmallows," warns the trail guide.

"Chittum," says the newt lady, pointing to the cascara. "That's what the Indians called it. The bark makes a strong laxative." The man walking with her nods in agreement. Another close call.

So put thoughts of a wienie roast out of your mind and continue downhill, through a grove of Port Orford cedars, their crowns so thick they block the light, turning day to dusk. "I'll bet it's cool in here on a hot day," says the man walking with the newt lady. But he doesn't warn about eating or roasting any part of the cedar.

Like the ponderosa pines that want to grow in a different region, these 50 year old cedars belong elsewhere—along a 200 mile stretch of coast that begins at Coos Bay in southwestern Oregon and reaches south to northwestern California. On this

Where to Go

•Peavy Arboretum is seven miles north of Corvallis off Highway 99W.

When to Go

•The arboretum is open for day use only.

•Some trails are open only seasonally, usually from April through October.

What to Expect

•One source says that "Human illness and death have resulted from ingesting live newts." But another says it "doesn't harm people but can sicken or kill small animals that eat it." So until they're sure, you might want to follow the newt lady's advice and avoid eating them—or at least brewing them with your coffee.

Things to Know

•The arboretum started in 1926 and was named for George W. Peavy, Oregon State University's first dean of the College of Forestry and one of the university's presidents.

•The biggest landowner of Oregon's forests is the federal government with 57%. Following are industrial landowners (21%), private landowners (16%) and state or local government (5%).

Who to Contact

•For more information, call the arboretum at 541-737-4434.

hillside the trees' shade and acidity knock out the understory and leave the ground bare. (Note: The characteristics of their needles and cones make all Oregon cedars false cedars; true cedars are native only to the Mediterranean and Himalayan regions.)

But once out of the cedar grove, the ground grows thick again as you enter a world of shrubs and streams, of moss and maples, of wildflowers and—

"Banana slug," the newt lady says.

Sure enough, there on the trail is the slick, yellow little fellow, a mollusk that uses its mucous slime to slide along forest floors.

"Don't eat it," the newt lady says. "The slime numbs the lips and tongue." The man walking with her nods in agreement. Another forest hazard avoided. But after crossing a bridge and wandering back toward the gravel road, you'll find the sign of a different danger.

"Cougar Notice," says the signpost on the edge of the road. Seems they've been spotting the big cats nearby. If you, too, should spot one, the sign's message advises you to "Maintain eye contact with the cougar. Do all you can to appear larger. Speak firmly in a loud voice." Oh my.

So puffing your chest and flailing your arms, as the sign advises, continue downhill, along a trickle of a stream passing through a shallow draw, and break out into the clearing, where picnic tables mark your return to civilization. At this point, you'll probably realize this has been no ordinary hike, for you've walked a forest path, breathed its air, met its trees, seen its future—and escaped its cougars, slugs, chittum, and newts.

Silver Falls

In a time not long ago, what is now one of the most beautifully wild areas in Oregon was a land unwanted, a place "absolutely bare except for hundreds or thousands of stumps that from a distance look like so many dark headstones." The time was the 1920s; the place, Silver Falls, located on the edge between the Willamette Valley and the Cascade Mountains. But then the times—and the land—changed.

From the 1880s until the 1930s, Silver Falls City sat near South Falls, a premier attraction of today's Silver Falls State Park, which one writer calls "one of the most beautiful places on the planet." For almost five decades, however, logging companies cut the canyons' cedars and firs to stumps. Forest fires took care of the rest.

When the timber disappeared, so did the town. By 1929, the last remaining family was charging spectators twenty-five cents each to watch cars run over 177-foot South Falls. Then the Great Depression hit, the government bought the land, and the Civilian Conservation Corps arrived to make the buildings, bridges, roads, and trails that you find in the park today.

With approximately 8,700 acres—more than 13 square miles—Silver Falls is Oregon's largest state park, a complex of picnic shelters, historical buildings, campgrounds, and trail systems found near the summit of a gently rolling road that takes you past oak groves, hay fields, and tree farms on your way to what's been called "The greatest concentration of waterfalls in the U.S." And the path that leads you through it is the Trail of Ten Falls.

This seven-mile loop has two segments—the Ridge Trail and the Canyon Trail. Perhaps the best starting point is the Canyon Trail's South Falls, the park's most visited area. From the trailhead, an asphalt path leads down the slope and passes behind the falls, where a white curtain of water makes the outside world seem misty and wet.

When you come out, follow the South Fork of Silver Creek into a world of soft and lacy green, of fronds and moss and leaves wavering with insects and wind. But you'll also find history in the stump of a cedar that was 400 years old when it was cut about 1900 by men using springboards, axes, and crosscut saws.

Down the trail is Lower South Falls. Descend the steps of rock and wood to the creek, then slip behind the falls, where the spray pounding the basalt makes the air quiver. From here the trail veers from Silver Creek's South Fork and toward its North Fork, a stream so clear that the water is a glassy ripple sliding past stones. Along this route are Lower North Falls, a 30-foot cascade, and Double Falls, at 178 feet the highest of the ten waterfalls.

"Gorgeous place, isn't it?" says a man hiking with his wife. He smells of aftershave and looks like Vincent Price. "It's too beautiful for words." His wife smiles and nods. It's a feeling that seems to fall like...er, water upon the people who visit here.

Hard to believe this is the same Silver Creek that was turned down twice for designation as a National Park—first in 1926 and again in 1935—because "the prevalence of cut over lands and farming activity...destroy(s) that feeling of nature...so essential to a National Park." But when the logging, grazing, and burning stopped, the land began to heal its wounds, cleaning its streams and reforesting its canyons.

Today things must look much as they did before the mills of Silver Falls City cut their first boards. Upstream past Drake Falls and Middle North Falls, the trail winds past firs and hemlocks, vine maple and Oregon Grape, salmonberry and salal. Alders and cottonwoods grow along the creek bottoms and, of course, streams of water plunge into the canyon, bouncing their roar off walls of basalt.

At Twin Falls the man who looks like Vincent Price sits on the bank and holds hands with his wife. Together they watch the water tumble past. A short distance up the trail, rocks the size of small barns, sprouting flowers and ferns and moss, squat in the stream.

Near the end of the Canyon Trail is North Falls, its water pounding the point of a rock that hunkers in the pool. Behind the falls is the maw of the canyon wall—the gaping mouth and the deep belly of rock, where Indian boys and girls once sought to complete their vision quests. Step inside this stone sanctuary and you might sense the same power.

Here inside the mountain, beneath the creek, and behind the falls is the rumble and splash of water, the thrumming pulse of the canyon. Tree casts dimple the rock overhead. These casts formed when lava covered an ancient forest, and the trees rotted, leaving their shapes in the rock. A bit of immortality.

Maybe the people who carve their names and their messages into the cavern's sitting benches are after the same thing. Their graffiti seems to say, "I was here, and my name will last unto the end of this bench." Well, you do what you can.

Climb the concrete stairway and its stone handrail away from the falls and out of the canyon, and you'll find the creek on top running fast with blue-green swirls, and the path leading to Upper

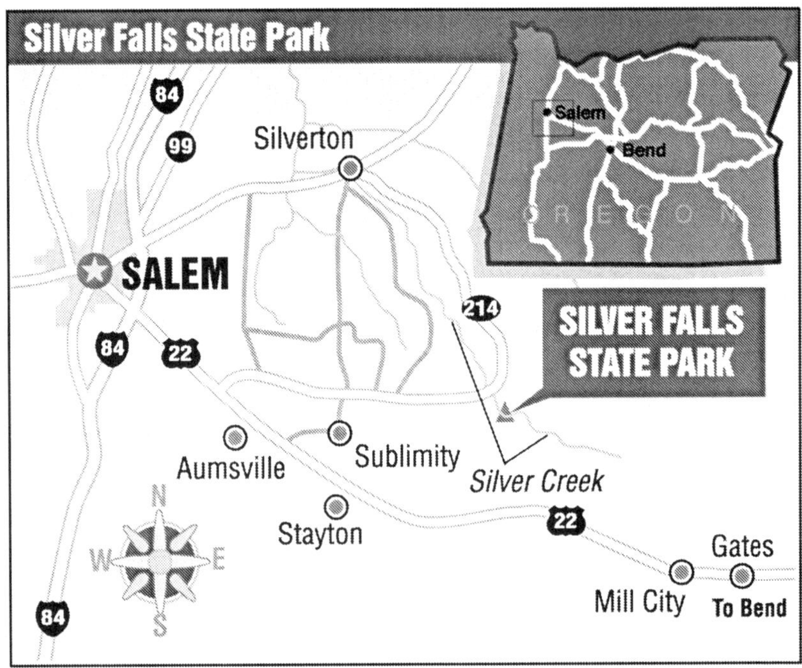

North Falls, a friendly pool at the end of your journey along the Canyon Trail.

To finish the loop, pick up the Ridge Trail and follow it for less than three miles back to South Falls. This is a hard-packed gravel path that runs parallel to the highway, winding past firs so thick it would take two or three people to give a single tree a decent hug.

The man who looks like Vincent Price wanders off this way, still holding hands with his wife. Deeper into the forest, the sound of falling water grows distant, then disappears, until the scrunch of gravel is the only sound left on the trail.

Where to Go

•From Salem, take Highway 22 toward Stayton and turn off at the exit for the Silver Falls Tour Route.

When to Go

•The park is open year-round, so take your pick of seasons—from the watery rush of spring to the calming silence of winter.

•The gate near the South Falls trailhead is open from 8 a.m. until 9 p.m. The trailheads at Winter Falls and North Falls don't have gates.

What to Expect

•Dogs and bikes are prohibited from the Canyon Trail.

Things to Know

•Between 200 and 300 people once lived in Silver Falls City.

•The CCC worked at Silver Falls from 1935 until 1942, using 200 men at a time in 14 six-month shifts.

•Silver Falls was dedicated as a state park in 1933.

Who to Contact

•For more information, call the park at 503-873-8681.

SOUTHWEST

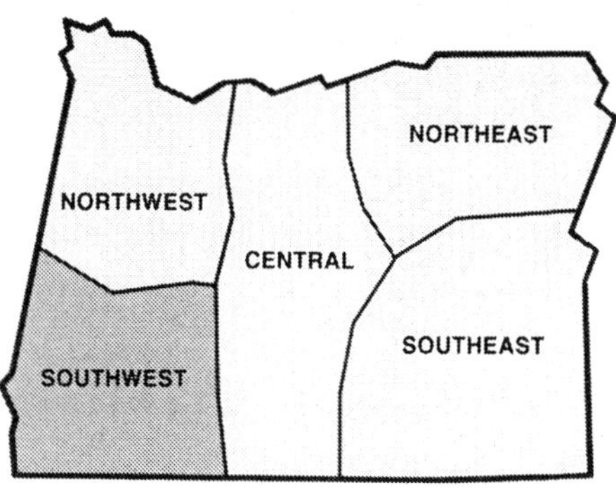

Oregon Dunes

It's a part of Oregon that refuses to hold still, that shifts and drifts then piles for miles along the coast, forming one of the Northwest's largest sandboxes. They put just one label on this 40 mile stretch of playground running from Florence in the north to Coos Bay in the south—the Oregon Dunes National Recreation Area (ODNRA). But the land itself is a wind-swept, wave-carved mosaic of nature, the pieces made from the forests and beaches, the streams and lakes that are spotted with campgrounds and crossed with trails.

"If you do *anything* outdoors," says a man visiting the area, "then you'll probably find what you're looking for somewhere along the Oregon Dunes."

The list of opportunities is long, especially when sung to the tune of *The Twelve Days of Christmas*—30 lakes for fishing, 14 trails for hiking, 13 places for camping, nine sites for picnicking, two platforms for viewing, and a partridge in a pear...oops. Well, the point is that this is a special place.

"The Oregon Dunes are the most extensive, and present the most spectacular dunal landscape on the Pacific Coast," says ODNRA headquarters. And one of the first questions many visitors want answered is this: Where the heck did all this sand come from?

The story of the dune's formation is a chapter from the book of the powers of the earth. Once long ago—12 million years or so—when most of Oregon was covered by ocean, the earth grew restless and began to rise, pushing the Coast Range above the surrounding sea. The sea retreated and the rivers followed, picking up pieces of the mountains along the way, tumbling the rocks along and wearing them down and finally turning stone into sand. But when the sea swallowed that sand, it decided it didn't like it—would you?—and waves swept it back onto the beaches.

From there it was the wind's turn, and for thousands of years it huffed and puffed and blew the sand inland for more than two miles, shaping it into the formations you see today. (The present shoreline is about 6,000 years old.) Depending on how the wind pushes and sculpts them, these dunes are classified as oblique, transverse, or parabola. To make life even more difficult for those who simply want to call a dune a dune and then go play on it, there are also foredunes and hummocks, deflation plains and tree islands.

"Oh, who cares about all that anyway?" says a woman visiting the area. "They're big and they're beautiful—go out and enjoy them."

Even though you don't have to be a duneologist to enjoy the place, the area is so vast—31,500 acres, almost 50 square miles—that the ODNRA has set up some easy ways to introduce its history, its land, and its wildlife to you. A couple of mile-long hiking trails, for example, can acquaint you with the basic character of the place. Both trails are located just off Highway 101. Eight miles south of Florence is the Taylor Dunes Trail, and 11 miles south of Reedsport is the New Umpqua Dunes Trail.

Perhaps the best site, however, is the Oregon Dunes Overlook, 10 miles south of Florence. Here you'll find viewing decks that provide long vistas of the dunes, interpretive signs that explain the natural and human history of the area, and trailheads that lead down onto the sand.

The main path from the overlook first leads through a tunnel of huckleberry and rhododendrons, coastal pine and Douglas fir, Sitka spruce and bracken ferns, then ends on the dunes, where posts point the way to other routes—the mile-long Overlook Beach Trail and the three-miles-long Tahkenitch Creek Trail. Yet many seem content to stay here and explore only this small section of sand.

"This is such a unique environment," says a woman on the dunes with her Labrador retriever. She points out where lupine and wild

strawberries sprout from the sand and where deer tracks cross it. In the distance, the ocean is a dim roar, and above it rises the buzz of hummingbirds. "It's always changing," she says. "You can visit it 20 times, and each time would be different, each time your footprints can be the first ones here."

The woman and her Lab are standing on the edge of a pond, one of many in thc area that demonstrates the diversity of the dune habitat. While sand blocked the streams and cut off ocean inlets to form the larger lakes, these ponds are most likely the result of sand depressions filling either with seasonal run-off or a rising water table.

Nearby is another contrast to the sand, though this one is fast becoming a problem—European beach grass. A hundred years ago, these dunes were almost completely bare of vegetation; as a result, they were unstable, the sand constantly drifting. So beach grass was planted to stabilize the dunes and protect the roads and channels from sand. It worked. Maybe too well.

The grass spreads so quickly and stabilizes so completely that it creates a foredune, a low hill running parallel to the ocean, which blocks the movement of sand inland. Because of this wall against the wind, the dunes are becoming static—yet it is their movement that keeps them alive. For this reason, the Oregon Dunes may have a limited life span.

"I have to believe they'll do something about it before it's too late," says a man at the overlook. "The sand is too beautiful to let the grass kill it." This is a much different attitude than that held by early Oregon settlers, who saw the dunes as a wasteland, in the beginning good only for stagecoach roads, and then later as a bombing range.

"The Oregon dunes are like no other sand dunes in the world," says ODNRA headquarters. "Desert-like landscapes, lakes, rivers, ocean and forest blend together, creating diverse ecosystems of plants and animals." And at the same time, it gives thousands of people the chance once again to play in the sand.

Where to Go

•Major access points are along Highway 101 from Florence in the north to Coos Bay in the south.

When to Go

•The visitors center in Reedsport is open daily in summer from 9-5, and during the other three seasons from 8-4:30 weekdays and 10-4 weekends.

What to Expect

•A day use charge of $3 per vehicle per day is in effect through the ODNRA. A $25 annual pass is also available.

•Be aware of vehicles on the beach and the dunes; they are permitted during designated times along established routes. 6,100 acres of the ODNRA, for instance, is open to vehicles.

Things to Know

•Offshore, the sand is 80-170 feet deep. Currents, tides, and waves carry smaller grained sands inland, while heavier grains remain on the beach.

Who to Contact

•For more information, call the ODNRA visitors center at 503-271-3611.

Oregon Vortex

The Indians of southwest Oregon once called it The Forbidden Ground. People today call it the Oregon Vortex. But no matter how the name changes, the mystery remains in a small creekside plot of land just outside southwest Oregon's Gold Hill.

Here balls roll uphill, brooms balance upright, and trees grow bent; people enlarge as they face north and shrink when they turn south, while birds avoid the place altogether. The reasons for the mysterious forces flowing through this land combine elements of physics, philosophy, and even magic. It all depends on how you look at it.

"I remember visiting here as a child," says a man at the vortex. "Back then I saw it as a fascinating curiosity, but now I see it as something of a puzzle without a solution."

For almost 70 years, the Oregon Vortex has shown parts of this puzzle to people who have come from all over the world to experience the weird world of a vortex, a place where lines of force are distorted, specifically where magnetic lines cross one another.

"A vortex is a force that spins around, like a whirlpool," says Nicholas R. Nelson, an authority on the area as well as one of its guides. "It's a universal structure, the basic form of the universe, from the largest galaxy to the smallest atom."

In the case of the Oregon Vortex, the affected area covers only three-quarters of an acre that is part of what was originally a 20-acre patent mining claim. The vortex itself is a sphere; more than half of it lies underground, yet its magnetic effects extend thousands of feet into the air, creating havoc with some aircraft instruments.

In addition, the vortex is covered by a protective corona, which serves as a shield. This structure, Nelson says, is comparable to an orange and its peel. "The corona encircles the vortex," he says, "seemingly holding the vortex in and keeping the normal world out." Surrounding him are madrone trees growing toward magnetic north, and an eerie silence created by the absence of birds.

Within the vortex, probably nothing demonstrates better how well the corona does its job of keeping out the normal world than the House of Mystery, a ramshackle, twisted building located close to the center of the vortex. The House began as an assay shack in 1904, then three years later slid down the hill and ended up where you see it today. Its mysteries include the balancing brooms and the uphill-rolling balls, as well as people and plumb bobs that seem to tilt at impossible angles.

"What causes it?" Nelson asks. "I sure don't know. But the visitors I like best are the debunkers." He explains that these are the skeptics, those who don't take appearances at face value, those who ask questions about what they see—or think they see. Even instruments—compasses, rulers, levels—don't always help you tell the difference because once inside the vortex, they are subject to its forces.

To demonstrate how this works, Nelson tells the story of the carpenter who came to repair some damage on the House of Mystery. After measuring the length of the board he needed, the carpenter went back to his truck, which was parked outside the vortex, and cut the board. When he returned to the House, the board was too short. Again he took the measurement inside the vortex and made the cut outside, and again the board was too short. After several attempts, he finally packed his saw into the vortex and cut the board there. It was a perfect fit.

Some people, of course, would find that this incident involved bad carpentry rather than inexplicable mystery. It's part of a controversy that's been going on for a long time. The first whites noticed the strangeness of this ground as early as 1864. But it wasn't until Scottish geologist and mining engineer John Litster

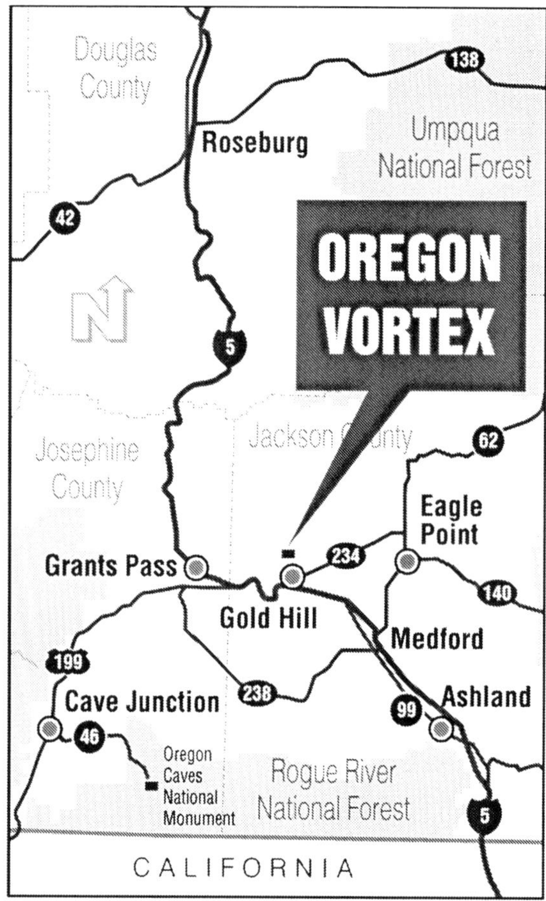

purchased the property in the late 1920s—he opened it for tours in 1930—before any scientific investigations were begun in the area.

Before Litster died in 1959, he had performed more than 14,000 experiments during more than 30 years of research. Whether that work yielded any answers to the vortex's phenomena is unknown, for Litster burned all his notes, saying, "The world is not ready for this knowledge."

Even so, theories abound. These include the idea that the vortex acts as a prism, refracting light to create visual distortions; that magnetic meteorites buried deep in the earth distort instrument readings; that the leaning building and trees create optical illusions; and that Albert Einstein's General Theory of Relativity is at work, which means the changes you see are actually taking place.

"I saw my husband shrink before my eyes," says a woman visiting the vortex. "First his nose was pressed against my forehead, but after we traded places [north for south] it was against my nose."

Perhaps this is where the philosophy comes in—with your view of the world and your reaction to seeing it changed. "If you think about it," Nelson says, "each of us is an eddy in the continuum of reality, like a rock in the stream of reality."

Once you step inside the Oregon Vortex, you might see that stream change as it bends around you. When you see that happen—or think you see that happen—you might find the best explanation for it on a sign nailed to the wall of the cabin sitting downhill from the House of Mystery—"We know practically nothing about anything."

Where to Go

•From Interstate 5 southwest of Grant's Pass, take Exit 43 or 40, then follow the signs for approximately four miles.

When to Go

•The Oregon Vortex is open from March until October, starting daily at 9:00 a.m. During summer months, the last tour begins at 5:15; during the rest of the year, 4:15.

What to Expect

•An illness similar to sea-sickness can strike some people who enter the House of Mystery.

Things to Know

•The House of Mystery may have more than 300 imitations around the country, though only two are built on vortexes. The others rely on optical illusions to achieve the vortex's effect.

•The only notes John Litster left behind are published in the booklet Notes and Data.

Who to Contact

•For more information, call the Oregon Vortex at 541-855-1543.

Shore Acres

My wife and I have a deal. If I take her to Shore Acres State Park, then she won't divorce me. Judging by the number of still-married couples strolling the pebbled-concrete paths at the park, many others have preserved their marital bliss by making the same deal. Even so, it's clear that some of these couples see the garden differently.

"This almost makes me cry," says a woman near the entrance.

"Why?" her husband says.

"It's so pretty."

"Oh."

She takes his arm and steers him along a row of English boxwood bordering the formal garden. Here beneath a coastal gray sky, a span of green boxes and rectangles lie spangled with tulip reds and daffodil yellows, though the show of flowers changes regularly during the growing season.

"People are always asking us about the best time to visit here," says a woman who belongs to the Friends of Shore Acres. "But anytime is the best time, depending on what you want to see."

So in this seven acre garden located southwest of Coos Bay, it's February and March for spring bulbs and daffodils, March and April for tulips, April and May for rhododendrons and azaleas, May through September for flowering annuals and perennials, and so on through roses and dahlias and into December, when they string thousands of Christmas lights through the garden to fill in the color-gaps left behind by missing or sleeping flowers.

"Every step reveals something new," the woman says to her husband as she steers him toward the Oriental garden. "It might be blossoms or flowers or water, maybe a stone or a bridge or a fence—but no matter where you go here, there's always something new to see."

"Oh," her husband says.

This design is no accident, for the garden was once part of the private estate of Louis Simpson, an heir to a lumber and shipping fortune. Simpson's father, Asa Simpson, was a Forty-niner who traveled from Maine to California in search of gold. He soon learned, however, that the big money was in timber rather than in gold, and in less than a decade his business was cutting and milling timber along the Oregon and Washington coasts, then shipping the lumber around the world.

In 1899, Louis arrived in Coos Bay to manage his father's businesses there. One day in 1905, while out in the woods with some timber cruisers, Simpson followed an abandoned trail to the cabin of a man named Jake Evans, and there he stopped for a cup of coffee.

"While we were resting in front of the shack, I caught a gleam of reflected light from the ocean," Simpson said. "It was a perfect day and the sun was shining gloriously." He decided to take a look around and found himself crawling through the dense underbrush.

"Finally, hot and breathless, I emerged upon a little open space," he said. "Immediately I saw what a place for a country home! I went back to the cabin and I said, 'Jake, did you ever think of selling?'" And so for $4,000, Louis Simpson bought Jake Evans' 320 acres, and within a year began building the house that would become the mansion of Shore Acres.

Paneled in myrtlewood, lit by Tiffany lamps, and carpeted with Persian rugs, the mansion grew from a summer home into a year-round residence for Simpson and his wife. Further remodeling and expansion turned it into one of the largest homes in Oregon at the time, with a ballroom larger than many family homes and a swimming pool just a bit smaller than the Pacific Ocean.

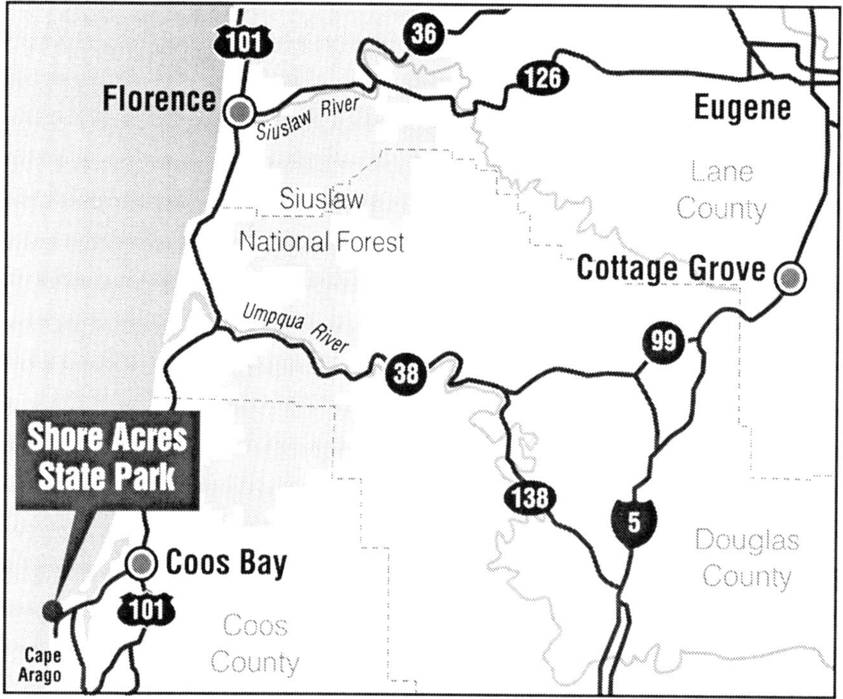

During this time, Simpson's ships were bringing back exotic trees and shrubs from their voyages around the world, and a crew of gardeners was kept busy planting them in a garden that would take three decades to create. Even when disaster struck in 1920 with the death of Mrs. Simpson, then again in 1921 with the burning of the mansion, the garden kept growing.

Although it's gone through many changes in its more than 80 years of life, the garden still contains parts of the original. The Oriental garden, for example, still has a gravel path, copper cranes, and pond lilies, just as it did in the days when Simpson and his guests played tennis on the nearby courts. In addition, the stones lining the pond are the cousins of the boulders that Simpson's crews hoisted from the beach cove to the cliff top with teams of horses. But much of the beauty here lies in gentle discoveries.

"Look at this," says the woman steering her husband by the arm. Almost hidden in the shadows and blossoms of the pond's trees, she points a slender finger toward a bamboo tube poking out of a rock, dripping water into a leaf-dappled pool of water held in the hollow of a moss-layered stone. The pool is the size of two palms held together side-by-side.

"I've read about it, heard about it," the woman says. "But it's not the same as being here. A photo just can't capture it. You get immersed in the sound of water and birds and squirrels. I'm just overwhelmed by it."

"Oh," her husband says. And once again she takes his arm and steers him away, oohing and ahhing over the scent and the sight of flowers as they wander off over spots of lawn that curve against shaggy screens of green. They pass by Oregon's largest Monterey pine, its limbs spreading to the sky and reaching for the light. Near it stands a Japanese plume cedar, its trunk bent and gnarled, its boughs lacy green.

The garden, however, makes up only seven of the park's more than 700 acres—the rest contains hiking trails, picnic areas, and

Where to Go

•From Coos Bay on Highway 101, follow the signs 13 miles southwest along the Cape Arago Highway.

When to Go

•The park is open year-round from 8 a.m. till dusk.

What to Expect

•Dogs are not permitted outside vehicles.

•A day use permit is required.

Things to Know

•The town of North Bend was created largely through the ideas, effort, and money of Louis Simpson.

•The 1921 fire that burned the Shore Acres mansion resulted in an estimated loss of $120,000, only half of which was insured.

•In 1918 Louis Simpson, known as "The Handsome Stranger," ran for governor on the Republican ticket. His campaign was based on "Develop Oregon" and "National Woman Suffrage."

•In 1948 the state razed the second Simpson mansion rather than pay for its maintenance.

Who to Contact

•For more information, call 503-888-3732.

beach access—for the Simpson estate once stretched for more than two miles along the coastline, from Sunset Bay in the north to Cape Arago in the south. In fact, after building a second mansion soon after the destruction of his first home, Simpson found the expense of the estate so great that in the 1930s he began donating and selling land to the state.

Then came four decades of tough times for the park; it housed troops in World War II, survived the winds of the Columbus Day storm in 1962, and battled years of neglect caused by budget problems. But Shore Acres began its rebirth in 1975, when a rededication ceremony marked the beginning of the park's rehabilitation into one of Oregon's premier garden spots.

Now as the day slides toward evening and the garden toward closing, the colors of the flowers change with the scud of clouds and the shift of light. The woman steering her husband toward the gate leans against his arm and says something that's carried away on a whiff of ocean breeze.

Her husband clears his throat. "If you like," he says, "we can come back again someday."

"Oh," she says, smiling. And then she nudges me out of the garden and toward the sound of waves.

South Slough

When William Wells, a New York writer, ventured into the Coos Bay country on an 1855 hunting trip, he found an unexpected world. "A motionless woods of giant growth and dark as a Gothic cathedral," is the way he described his discovery. But as his party continued its horseback trip through the South Slough of Coos Bay, Wells worried about "the probable time when the advance of civilization should sweep away this cloud of foliage..."

Even though civilization staked its claim and took its toll on South Slough, the land was so isolated and rugged that in 1974—119 years after Wells' trip—the slough became the nation's first Estuarine Sanctuary. Now protected in a National Estuarine Research Reserve (NERR), South Slough holds more than seven square miles of what has been called "one of the richest places on earth."

This wealth is measured in terms of the life that thrives in an estuary, which is a place where a river meets the sea. The mixing of fresh water with salt water creates one of the most productive environments on earth, attracting and supporting a tremendous variety and number of life forms—including human beings. As a result, cities now sit on the shores of virtually every major estuary in the country. South Slough, however, is different.

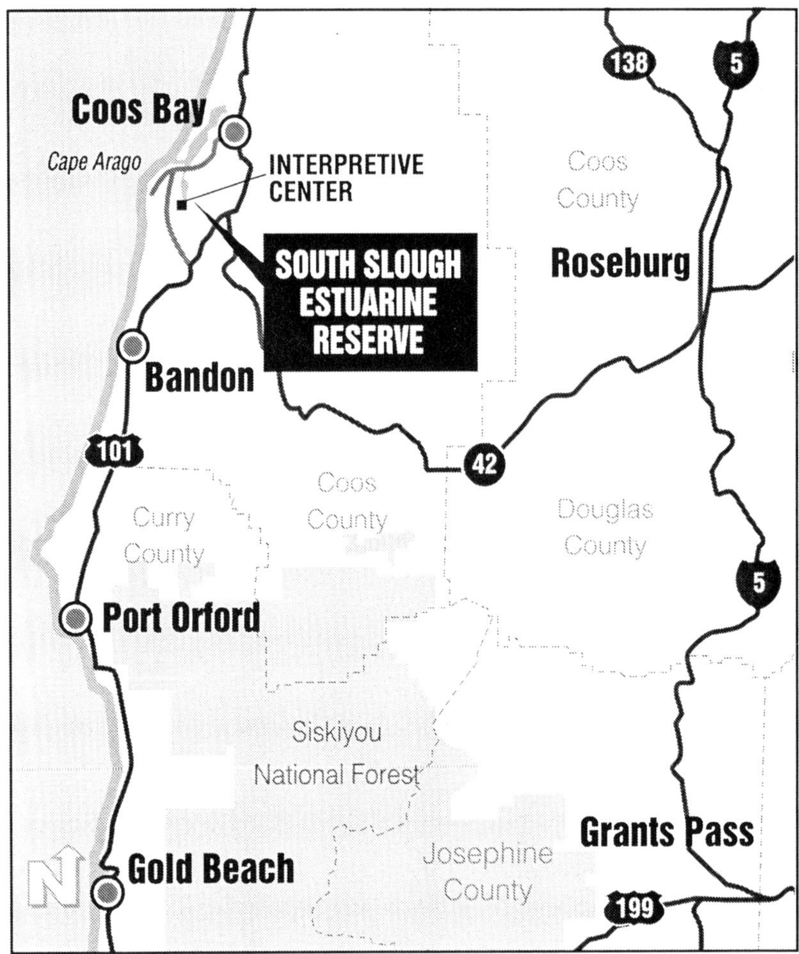

"South Slough remains one of the few estuaries in the Northwest to have escaped such development," says the NERR. "It offers a rare opportunity to visit an estuary still close to its wild and natural state."

To help you in your visit, South Slough offers a network of trails that leads through forest, meadows, and marsh. These include short loop trails that provide an overview of the area as well as a handicap-accessible trail. But the route that takes you through the widest range of habitats is the Hidden Creek Trail, a three mile round-trip journey that follows the stream from the uplands to the estuary.

The trail begins near the creek's headwaters and winds downhill through a 75 acre watershed, dropping 100-feet to the creek itself, then another 200-feet to the sea level edge of the estuary. Through the scent of cedar and near the splash of water you'll travel, past benches and over footbridges, their stringers trimmed to nudge past the bumps and branches of logs. Soon you'll reach a sign pointing the way to the slough via the Skunk Cabbage Walk.

"This is one of the darndest things I've ever seen," says a man walking along a boardwalk, a path of planks elevated above the floppy green leaves of skunk cabbage. The leaves, which are the size of small children, crowd along the edges and lean over the sides of the boardwalk.

"This seems to be part of the whole attitude here," says the man's wife, who's following one of the boardwalk's viewing loops around an alder tree. "You get right into the center of things, become part of it without damaging it."

The woman, who turns out to be a skunk cabbage scholar, says the plant's name has tarnished its reputation, and explains that the Indians boiled its roots to make a cough syrup, rubbed its leaves on their skin to fend off mosquitoes, and used its juices to treat poison

Where to Go

• From Charleston, located eight miles southwest of Coos Bay, take Seven Devils Road south for four miles.

When to Go

• Interpretive center hours 8:30-4:30 weekdays from September through May, and daily from June through August.

What to Expect

• Trail guides and brochures are available at the interpretive center.

Things to Know

• The South Slough Reserve contains 3,855 acres of upland forest, 800 acres of tidelands, and 115 acres of freshwater habitat, for a total of 4,770 acres.

• Each year over 3,000 students participate in educational projects at South Slough.

Who to Contact

• For more information, call 541-888-5558.

oak rash. But even she is surprised by the skunk cabbage encountered along this trail. "Its size and color and density—everything about its growth here is remarkable."

When the boardwalk emerges from the skunk cabbage patch, it skirts a marsh and enters a forest at the estuary's edge. Here you'll find rhododendrons climbing as high as 20 feet and huckleberries about half that. Nearby is a viewing platform you can climb to look out toward the waters of South Slough. This is the southwest arm of the larger Coos estuary, which is classified as a drowned river estuary. These began forming along the Oregon coast 20,000 years ago, when the glaciers began melting and the seas rising.

If you stayed here long enough to watch the rising and falling of the tide, you'd see how the sea makes soup—add salt to streams, stir well with currents and wind, bake with sunlight, then let the critters take over. First one-celled plants (phytoplankton) eat the soup, then small animals (zooplankton) eat the plants, then bigger animals eat the smaller...well, you know how it goes from there.

Soon the food chain reaches its people-populated peak, a condition familiar to South Slough for 5,000 years, beginning with the Miluk people. Archeologists have identified three major villages that once existed in the South Slough area. Each contained approximately 100 people who lived in cedar plank lodges either along the slough's shore or within the rain forest.

Even though these fishing, hunting, and gathering people were followed by trappers, miners, farmers and loggers, the signs of human-wrought changes in the slough are far less than at other estuaries in the country, one of the reasons for South Slough becoming the nation's first Reserve. According to Friends of South Slough, "It was felt that the area would gradually return to a natural, almost pristine, state."

Today that process continues. Logging and mining have stopped, buildings razed, and pastures abandoned; the dikes that blocked the tides and the ditches that drained the marshes are eroding. The animal life that calls this place home include some species that are listed or nominated as threatened or endangered, including bald eagles, peregrine falcons, brown pelicans, western snowy plovers, sea-run cutthroat trout, and coho salmon.

For a closer look at how the slough is healing, take the Tunnel Trail from near the viewing platform and follow it for a half-mile until you reach a restroom. This is the halfway point of the three-mile route, and from here you can head down to the water's edge, where you'll find a few marshside trails as well as a shoreline platform on which you can take a snooze in the sun. Across the way are some old railroad pilings; in the distance is a house. Yet little else remains of the slough's days of facing development.

"Since they had pushed all the brush off and cut all the trees," said a man who had lived in the area for most of his life, "it's time we did something to save South Slough."

It seems to have been a decision that most people agreed with, even those who had long worked the land and the woods and the waters of the slough.

Table Rocks

The Rogue River Valley of southwestern Oregon is a land with a violent past. Volcanoes have formed its terrain and war has shaped its history. The place where these two forces seem to meet is outside Medford at Table Rocks, two horseshoe-shaped mesas that loom so high above the valley floor that they're sometimes called "islands in the sky."

The story of Table Rocks begins almost 10 million years ago. Back then, the Rogue River was meandering along through its sandstone canyon, minding its own business, when the nearby Cascade Mountains erupted. This eruption filled the Rogue's canyon with andesite, a volcanic rock so hard that as time passed and the old sandstone on either side of the canyon began eroding, the andesite remained to mark the ancient riverbed. Eventually the Rogue's old channel was left towering some 800 feet above the surrounding valley. This phenomenon of turning a valley into a mountain is called inverted topography, and a hike to the top of either Table Rock will take you back to the ancestral course of the old Rogue River.

"The trail on Upper Table Rock is shorter by a quarter-mile and less steep," says a woman along the trail. "And that's important to someone my age." In her 70s, the woman wears a straw hat and carries a plant-identification book. She explains that Table Rocks' names come from their locations along the river. "Upper Table is upstream, Lower Table downstream."

The first stop on the mile-and-a-half, 750-foot climb to the top of Upper Table Rock is the trailhead sign, which warns about the ruggedness of the land you're about to enter. Although you probably won't see the rattlesnakes and ticks it describes, you will most definitely be keeping close company with some of the thickest and most widespread poison oak you'll ever encounter.

In fact, probably the only growth you'll find more luxuriant than the poison oak are the flowers. "This is a great wildflower walk," says a woman along the trail without her Labrador retriever. (Dogs are prohibited here.) "I've seen 20 different kinds of flowers, though I can't name them all." She does, however, list larkspur, lupine, lilies, buttercups, and Indian paintbrush among the morning's tally.

Far below, beyond the clusters of wildflowers and the tangles of chaparral, runs the river. Because it's near one of Medford's industrial areas, one side of the valley shows pastures and mountains; the other, smoke stacks and sewer lagoons. So while one side moos, the other honks. As a man along the trail says, "Just the road getting here takes you through the darndest mix of sawmills and pear orchards."

Along the slope itself, oak and pine and madrone grow side by side, much of it stunted or gnarled, fighting to grow in the dryness and the heat of an area that records some of the state's highest summertime temperatures. Nearer the top, firs take over, and the grade sharpens into its final ascent to the cap-rock. On top you'll find the oaks and pines and madrones—even a cedar or two—growing tall and straight, as though their roots remember the flow of water here. Remember—you're standing on stone that once cradled a stream.

Now a short walk across cobbled ground takes you along the ancient riverbed to the edge, where you can see the other side of this U-shaped mesa, as well as sliced ridges and misted mountains. The smoke rises and a haze drifts across a valley that sometimes seems to breathe with the sounds of truck brakes and diesel trains. And through that haze and downstream of the Rogue stands Lower Table Rock.

"Once when I was hiking up Lower Table Rock with a friend, I told her that the Indians made their last stand here," says the woman in the straw hat. "And just as I said it, she looked down on the trail

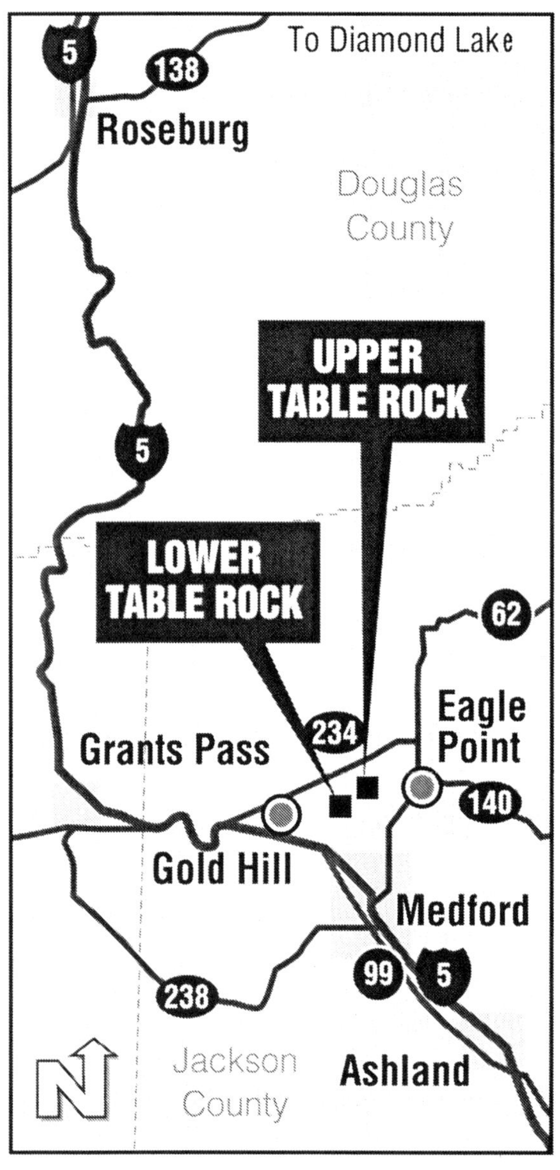

and found an arrowhead."

That last stand is another chapter in the valley's story. This one beginning with the people who called themselves the Takelma, but whom the whites named the Rogues.

The name came from nineteenth-century French trappers, who found the Takelma "a particularly troublesome lot." So they called them *Les Coquin*—thc Rogues, a term that attached itself to the river and the valley of the Takelma.

The problem began with the land. Without asking permission, miners crossed it on their way to the gold fields; without negotiating treaties, Congress divided it into homestead claims; and without paying compensation, settlers turned it into their farms, fields, and towns. Yet the Takelma wouldn't let it go without a fight.

"Never has an Indian country been invaded with better success or at a better time," Joseph Lane wrote in 1851. Lane had been Oregon's first territorial governor before serving as a brigadier-general of volunteer troops during the Rogue River war. His letter added, however, that the Takelma "gave me a terrible account of the invasion of their country by our people...that they were now afraid to lay down to sleep, for fear the white people would be upon them before they would awake, that they were tired of war and wanted peace." Yet that had to wait for two more years.

Then on a September day in 1853, the Takelma gathered at Lower Table Rock and asked for a peace council. Lane, who had been wounded during a recent battle with the Takelma, agreed to go, accompanied by only ten unarmed men. Waiting for him at Table Rock were 700 warriors.

"[I] told the general that...they were notoriously treacherous, and had earned the designation of 'Rogues' by never permitting a white man to escape with his scalp, when once within their power," said the man who accompanied Lane as interpreter, "and that it was folly for eleven unarmed men to place themselves voluntarily in the power of 700 well-armed hostile Indians, in their own secure encampment." Lane went anyway.

Today as you walk toward the top of Lower Table Rock, you'll find yourself where Lane stood that morning—in the midst of 700

Where to Go

•From Interstate 5, take Exit 32 near Medford. Go east one mile to Table Rock Road. For Upper Table Rock, turn right on Modoc Road and drive less than two miles to the parking area; for Lower Table Rock, turn left on Wheeler Road and drive less than a mile to the parking area.

What to Expect

•Neither trail has potable water.

Things to Know

•Joseph Lane was an Indiana Democrat and former Mexican War general when President James K. Polk appointed him Oregon's first territorial governor. After his service in the Rogue River wars, he served as one of Oregon's first U.S. senators before running for vice president on a pro-slavery Democratic ticket during the election in which Abraham Lincoln was elected president.

Who to Contact

•For more information, contact the Medford BLM office at 541-770-2385 warriors, cliffs looming behind them, troops waiting on the plain below. Then just as Lane and the Takelma were about to reach an agreement, a warrior rode into the camp with the news that some whites along Applegate Creek had murdered an Indian. Some of the Takelma demanded revenge.

"But what good will our blood do you?" Lane told them. "Our murder will exasperate our friends and your tribe will be hunted from the face of the earth. Let us proceed with the treaty, and in place of war have everlasting peace."

The peace they made that day lasted for only a couple of years; the Takelma as a free people, for not much longer. Table Rocks are still there, though, standing as symbols of the violent upheavals that changed the lives of both the river and its people.

CENTRAL

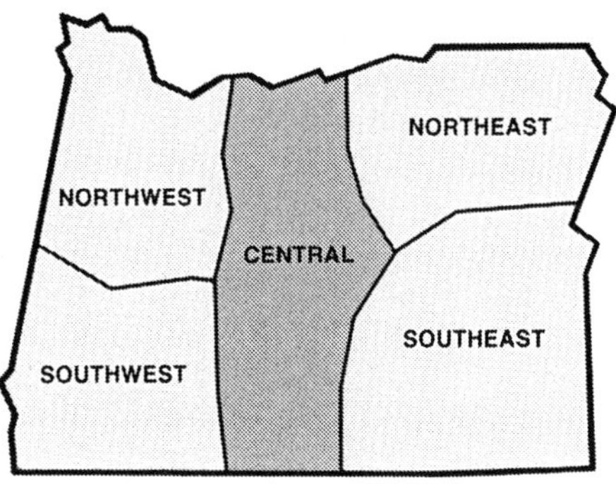

Beacon Rock

Even though Lewis and Clark saw it first, you can still do something those legendary explorers didn't even attempt: climb to the top of Beacon Rock, a landmark along the Columbia Gorge ever since members of the expedition first sighted it, just five days away from their date with the Pacific Ocean.

"In the meadow to the right, and at some distance from the hills stands a high perpendicular rock, about eight hundred feet high, and four hundred yards around the base," says part of the expedition's journal entry for November 2, 1805. "This we called the Beacon rock."

For more than a hundred years following Lewis and Clark's sighting, this chunk of basalt—once the neck of an ancient volcano that has been worn away by the river's erosion—was a craggy guidepost for travelers along the river. Then in 1915, a man named Henry Biddle, whose ancestor edited the first edition of the Lewis and Clark Journals for publication in 1814, bought the rock. But he wanted it to be more than just a Columbia Gorge curiosity.

So in October of that year his crews began building a trail to the top, up the almost vertical wall of jags and crevices that sprout grass, brush, and trees. And on an April day three years later, he finished it. In its time, the pathway was a marvel of both engineering and spending.

"This rock has a base covering about 12 acres of ground and stands about 850 feet above sea level," says a 1923 auto-tour guide of the Columbia Gorge."You will note a trail winding up its precipitous sides which is nearly 4,500 feet in length and built at a cost in excess of $10,000 by the owner of the rock, Mr. Henry J. Biddle."

After Mister Biddle died, his son and daughter gave the rock to the state of Washington in 1935. Today it stands as a state park, located approximately seven miles downriver from the Columbia River's Bridge of the Gods near Cascade Locks, Oregon. So if you want to feel a bit smug about seeing something that our most famous explorers missed, go to the park and climb to the top. The rock is the same as when Lewis and Clark saw it; the trail, as when Henry Biddle built it.

In the beginning, the trail is wide and smooth with an even grade. It takes you through the shade of a forest, past stone benches and bridges and walls. At about the five minute mark, you reach a gate and the ascent steepens. From here on up, the route is wrapped with steel railing or bridged with wooden planks as it climbs the switchbacks to the summit.

The path takes you in a spiral from sun to shade and then back again, the air hanging warm against you, and then cool as you step past a maze of handrails. You'll also find along this wall-hugging route an occasional stray rock that has leaped from the sides to squat ponderously on the trail.

Along the way you'll see spread out below and into the distance a long, slack stretch of Columbia River, a sweep of water and rock, of power lines and irrigation ditches, of tugboats and sailboats, barges and trains. But keep an eye out for dogs.

"There are more dogs than people out here," says a man strolling back toward the parking lot. Behind him, a blind Brittany seems to be feeling the trail with her paws as she limps down the rock-strewn switchback. "It was easier going up," says the woman guiding her.

At the summit is a rocky point overlooking the islands and channels of the Columbia, a fat serpent of a river, its sun-sparkling water dragging around the bends. In the distance is the whoosh of traffic, the rumble of trains, the hiss of air brakes along the

Interstate. This is another part of the Columbia that Lewis and Clark missed:

"Just below (Beacon Rock) is an Indian village of nine houses, situated between two small creeks. At this village the river widens to nearly a mile in extent, the low grounds too become wider, and they as well as the mountains on each side are covered with pine, spruce-pine, cottonwood, a species of ash, and some alder. After being so long accustomed to the dreary nakedness of the country above, the change is as grateful to the eye, as it is useful in supplying us with fuel."

Gone is the Indian village and its houses, gone the wild river and its untamed mountains; but still here is a deep and penetrating view of the forests, ridges, and water that is part of the River of the West.

At the summit, the pinnacle giving you this viewpoint is narrow and confined, which makes it likely that people will talk when they can no longer ignore one another. A man lights a cigarette and gazes out at the gorge. "Waterfalls," he says, "hiking trails—it's just spectacular."

"But I'm afraid of heights," his wife says, "so I almost had a heart attack coming up here."

"But the trail isn't nearly as far as you'd think, looking at it from the bottom," says another woman. She glances at her watch. "It only took a half hour."

"I like it better than Disneyland," says a young girl who made the hike in sandals and a flower-print dress.

"And the lines are shorter," says the man who seems to be the girl's grandfather.

But soon the power of the Gorge takes hold, and the summit of Beacon Rock falls into silence, for those who have made the climb to the top seem to realize they're experiencing something special—something that even Lewis and Clark missed.

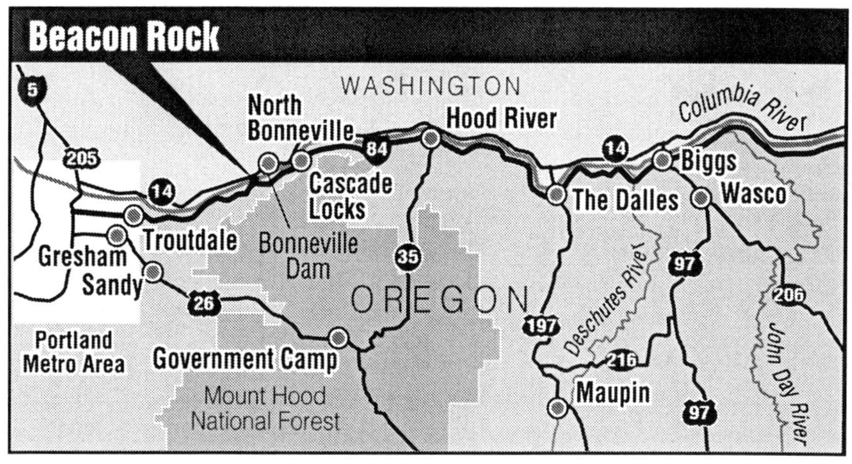

Where to Go

•From Interstate 84, take Exit 44 at Cascade Locks, then cross the Bridge of the Gods and drive west on Highway 14 for seven miles.

What to Expect

•Although a sign along the trail says rock climbing is prohibited at the park, another source calls it a location "favored by climbers...the south face offers more than 60 routes of varied difficulty." Go figure.

•The Bridge of the Gods is a toll bridge—75 cents per car, please.

Things to Know

•Officially, Beacon Rock is 848 feet tall; the more famous Crown Point is 725 feet.

•As you cross the Bridge of the Gods, watch the river for remnants of the old locks and canal, and for the Indian fishing platforms.

Captain Jack's Stronghold

Above the lava plain in the stone-broken land along the Oregon-California border, above a ground tilted with slopes and carved with ravines, a single medicine flag stands. Its staff might be only a dead juniper gripping the rocks, its banner only a cluster of cloth and feathers fluttering in the wind, but its spirit belongs to the Modoc Indians, as the land once did. The most dramatic and tragic chapters of the Modoc story, however, begin with the usual plot, involve the usual characters.

The time is the mid-nineteenth century; the place, the Klamath Basin of southern Oregon, a land of marshes, forests and mountains, and for thousands of years the ancestral home of the Modoc Indians. Then into this country move the settlers who either fear the tribe or want its land. As a result, the politicians bend to the pressure, and the Modocs move to the reservation. But then the plot turns—the Modocs flee, the cavalry pursues, and a war begins.

If you'd like to follow the trail of this story through its battlefield, then come along to Captain Jack's Stronghold, a lava labyrinth in northern California, where 125 winters ago, 50 Modoc warriors and their families fought the United States Army to a standoff.

The man who has come through history as the representative of both his people and their struggle is a Modoc named Kientpoos, whom the whites called Captain Jack. It was an 1864 treaty that put Captain Jack and his people on the Klamath Reservation near today's Klamath Falls, but it was a simmering feud that triggered the problems. They just didn't get along with the more numerous Klamath Indians, an adversary for the previous two centuries.

So after five years of harassment from both the Klamaths and the government, more than 300 Modocs in three bands left the reservation and returned to their homeland along the Lost River. For the next couple of years, nobody bothered them. But in late November of 1872, a cavalry company rode into the Modoc camp and ordered them back to the reservation. The Modocs resisted, fighting erupted, and the war started. Although some Modocs returned to the reservation, approximately 160 others fled to the lava beds. And in this land of volcanic fissures and cracks and caves, they waited for the war to find them.

Although the end of that war, like its beginning, is predictable in that the outgunned and outnumbered Modocs eventually surrendered, the fighting of it involved courage and tragedy, sacrifice and betrayal. And as it began to unfold during the winter of 1873, newspapers and magazines across the nation as well as in Europe described the struggle of the Modocs, the assassination of

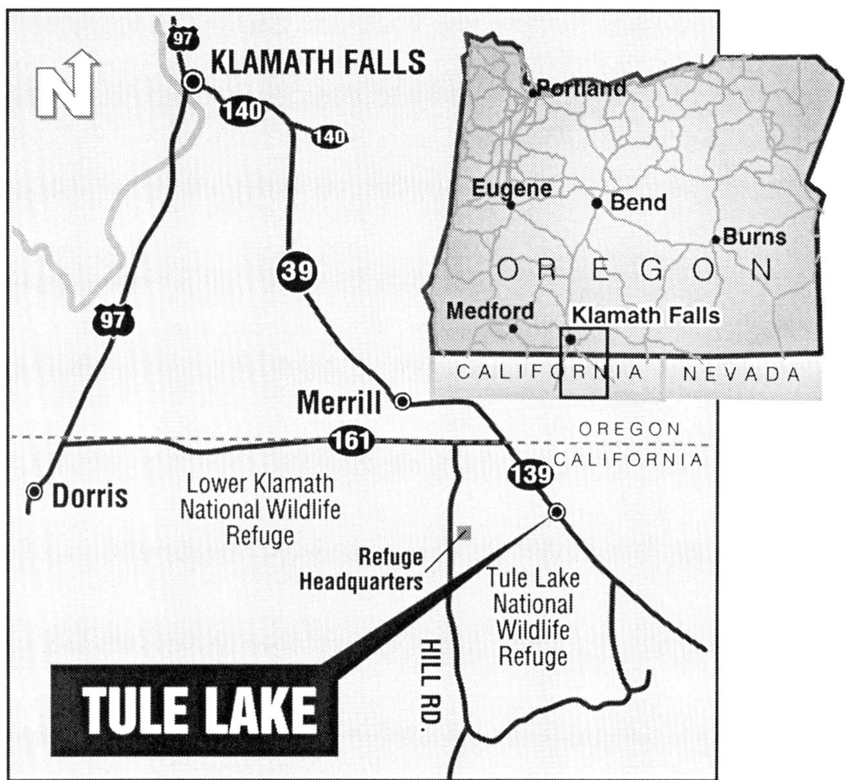

a general, the surrender of Captain Jack, and the imprisonment and hangings of the Modoc leaders.

Along the paths that now wind through what is known as Captain Jack's Stronghold, located on the edge of California's Lava Beds National Monument, you will find an eerie stillness, as though time is as rock-rigid as the lava, for here are the caves that sheltered the Modocs from winter, the walls that shielded them from bullets.

A looping trail system, which contains 23 marked sites, guides you through the battlefield that the Modocs called home during the winter of 1872-73. You'll step past their outposts and shelters, their defense lines and command posts; you can stand where the chiefs made decisions, where the warriors built fortifications, and where the people raised medicine flags for their magical powers and built dance rings for the spiritual strength they believed would help them defeat their enemies. But it was the lava itself that gave them their greatest military advantage.

"Textbooks don't do the place justice," says a woman on the trail. She gazes out over the lava maze that was an impenetrable fortress to army troops. "Even though I've read about the war and the battlefield," she says, "I could never imagine what it was like until I saw it."

Neither could the army. From a distance, the land seems flat and even, an easy walk or ride across gentle, open terrain. "It began with the army smugly optimistic," writes the great-granddaughter of one of the Modoc war chiefs. "Quite clearly, the soldiers expected to kill or capture every Modoc who had moved to the lava beds."

And so on a foggy January morning in 1873, Colonel Frank Wheaton led the army's first assault against the Stronghold, a two day battle that saw over 300 soldiers attack the 160 Modocs. Of these, approximately 50 were warriors. The result was 37 casualties for the army, none for the Modocs. In addition, the Modocs were able to salvage the rifles and ammunition dropped by fleeing soldiers.

"I have never before encountered an enemy occupying a position of such great natural strength," Colonel Wheaton said after the battle. "One of our men was wounded twice during the day, but

Where to Go

•From Klamath Falls, drive southeast on Highway 39 to the edge of the Lava Beds National Monument.

What to Expect

•An excellent guide to the Stronghold is available at the trailhead.

•Two trails loop through the Stronghold—a mile-and-a-half Long Trail, and a half-mile Short Trail.

Things to Know

•The Modoc war was the most costly war "per enemy" that the United States had fought to that point. Battle deaths were 69 whites and eight Modocs.

•Captain Jack and three other Modocs were hanged at Fort Klamath on October 3, 1873. Two others were sent to Alcatraz prison. 153 were exiled to Oklahoma.

Who to Contact

•For more information, call the Lava Beds National Monument at 530-667-2282.

he did not see an Indian at all." Wheaton also stated in his report that he thought it would take at least 1,000 men to defeat the Modocs.

As a result of their embarrassing defeat, the army bolstered itself with reinforcements, howitzers, and mortars, then attempted to negotiate a settlement. But this, too, backfired. At one of the peace conferences, the Modocs shot three of the peace commissioners, killing a general and a minister, and wounding the Indian agent. The war was on again.

The army's side of this war is also represented at the Stronghold, for here you can see the remains of the bivouacs, outposts, and fortifications built by young soldiers in a strange land, fighting a people they didn't even know and couldn't often see. "I never realized what a horrible thing war is, until I came out on this trip," wrote a second lieutenant stationed at Gillem's Camp, the army post built near the Stronghold and named for the campaign's first commanding officer.

The old camp site is the location of one of the two formal monument's dedicated to the army's cause. The other is Canby's Cross, which marks the spot where Captain Jack assassinated General E.R.S. Canby during the April peace conference. It was the act that pushed the Modoc leader beyond the point of no return.

By fighting and fleeing, the Modocs remained free until late spring. But hunger, exhaustion, and desperation finally split the bands, and the Modocs turned against one another. Captain Jack surrendered on the first day of June 1873, six months after the first shots were fired in the Modoc camp on Lost River.

"They scared me when they came to where I was living on Lost River and started this fight," Captain Jack said at his trial. "I cannot understand why they were mad with me." But Captain Jack could not save his people. The war leaders were hanged or imprisoned, the families exiled, their land taken away.

Today what is left of their struggles is the broken ground of lava and sage that holds the memory of their battles against overwhelming odds. And above this land rises a single medicine flag, which some say represents the idea that this place still belongs to the Modocs. As Captain Jack said when he argued that at least the lava beds should be left for his people—"Nobody will ever want these rocks."

Celilo Falls

It's one of the most beautiful and important places you'll never see, a wonder of history and geology and culture that is hidden from the thousands of travelers who pass by every day—Celilo Falls. And it's hiding place is deep beneath the dam-blocked waters of the Columbia River.

Lake Celilo they call it today. 12 miles upstream from The Dalles Dam. 24 miles of slack water on the edge of a park and near a village that carry the same name. But even though the falls itself lies in ghostly silence and lives only in memories and photographs, the park is worth visiting for the story it holds about the way Oregon and its people used to be.

The park sprawls across what was once the ancient fishing grounds of the tribes living along the middle stretch of the Columbia River. For generations these grounds were the center of a world that drew travelers and traders from as far away as California and Canada, the Great Basin and the Rocky Mountains. Here, near the roar of water tumbling over basalt, less than 200 miles from the mouth of the Columbia River, people gathered to swap the gadgets and gear, the trappings and tackle and tools that made this area the hub of one of the most complex cultures in the Northwest.

Geology tells us that this was a land formed after the volcanoes spewed forth the stuff of the earth, and the basalt came to shape the earth and the floods to carve the river. And where water and rock met there formed the great falls that came to be called the Cascades, the Dalles, and Celilo. Mythology, however, tells a different story.

One Indian legend says that once upon a time there was no Columbia River. Instead, a long ridge of mountains separated a great lake in the east from an ocean to the west. Seeing that the people who lived east of the ridge needed food, Coyote dug a hole through the mountains, and the lake poured through the hole and ran to the ocean, and the salmon swam up the stream and reached the people of the new river. Then when Coyote began to fancy some of the tribes' women, he repaid those who married him by creating rapids where the people could catch fish. One of these wedding gifts was Celilo.

When Lewis and Clark passed through Celilo on their way to the Pacific in 1805, they found a river a quarter-mile wide turning on edge to squeeze through a chute of basalt. "The whole of the Current of this great river must be at all Stages pass thro' this narrow channel of 45 yards wide," William Clark wrote.

After taking a 20-foot plunge—the height of a two-story building—at a speed Captain Clark estimated to be at least 30 miles an hour, the rapids roared and churned their way for another 14 miles downstream. Near one salmon fishing area, Clark "counted 107 stacks of dried pounded fish in different places on those rocks which must have contained 10,000 [pounds of salmon]." And this was in October, a time of low-water and past the peak of fishing season.

This kind of fishing lasted well into the next century, with salmon and steelhead sliding and leaping through the Celilo rapids on their journeys to spawning grounds as far away as 1,000 miles up the Columbia and its tributaries. In 1888, John Muir described the salmon run he witnessed as "countless millions, urging their way against falls, rapids, and shallows, up into the very heart of the Rocky Mountains, supplying everybody by the way with most bountiful masses of delicious food, weighing from twenty to eighty pounds each, plump and smooth like loaves of bread ready for the oven."

But after we turned the corner on the old century and headed into the new, changes came to the river and its fish. In 1905, a hundred years after Lewis and Clark first saw Celilo, the U.S. Army

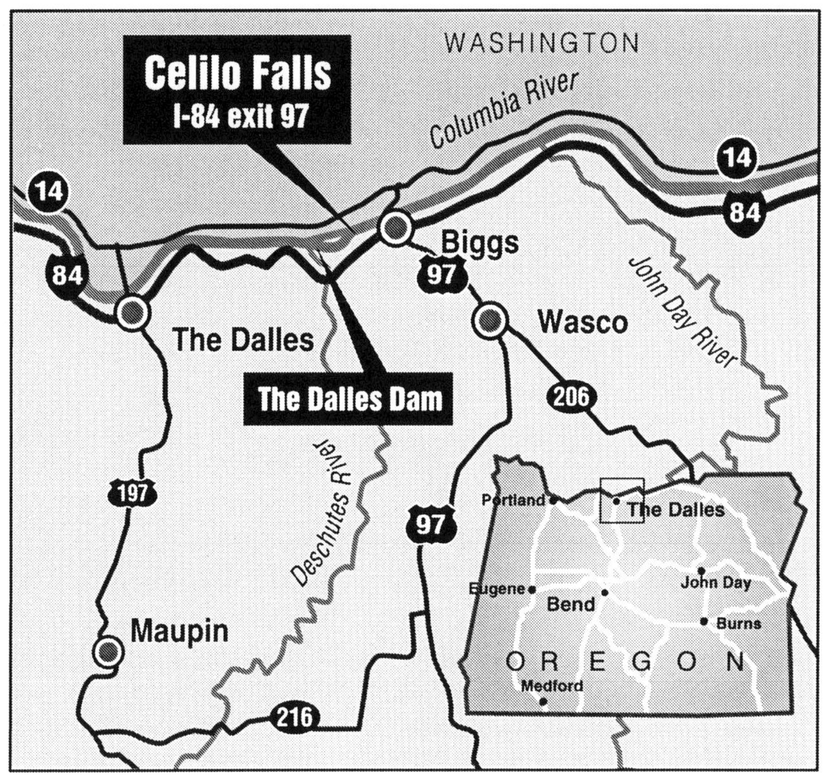

Where to Go

•Approximately 12 miles east of The Dalles on Interstate 84, take Exit 97.

Things to Know

•Some say Celilo was once named Wyam Falls; others, Tumwater or Tum Tum, for the sound of a heartbeat. But the origin and meaning of Celilo is uncertain.

•As compensation for the loss of their fishing grounds, the Yakima, Nez Perce, Umatilla, and Warm Springs tribes each received between 3 million and 10 million dollars, depending on what the government determined to be their loss.

•Indian fishing rights on the Columbia were granted, and are protected, by an 1855 treaty.

Corps of Engineers began building The Dalles-Celilo Canal, which permitted boats to navigate through the rapids. Ten years later they finished it. More changes came with the construction of the Columbia Gorge Highway and then Bonneville Dam. Yet the village of the people who fished at Celilo survived.

"I remember the village when I first saw it in the 1930s," writes Ralph Friedman, an Oregon author. "Crowded, alive, crackling with laughter, humming with the healthy sounds of happy work. That was when Indians were still fishing, as they had for centuries, from the cliffs above Celilo Falls...If the salmon were plenty, the long house shook with the beat of drums, the jangle of bells, the thud of dancing feet, the measured striking of hands, and the warm gales of laughter."

Then the laughter ended. The U.S. government decided to build a dam 12 miles downriver from the village. It meant the end of the fishing grounds. "The people here were pretty mad when they had to quit fishing at Celilo Falls," said a man who once lived at the village. "I was one of them mad—but I couldn't do anything. No one could."

So in 1952 the Yakima, Nez Perce, Umatilla, and Warm Springs tribes sold their part of the river to the U.S. government, and the village of Celilo was moved above flood level. In 1957, The Dalles Dam stood ready. The gates closed, the river pooled, the falls drowned—and the village of Celilo seemed to drown with it.

"The village lay inert under tawny rock cliffs scowling down upon rusty sage which sagged, dusty and exhausted, all through the settlement," Friedman writes. "Weathered rocks, looking like mud had drip-dried on their faces, were glazed eyes fixed upon junked cars dragged into the open to die and be stripped of their organs. If they had been flesh, the buzzards would have picked them clean to the bone. There appeared to be at least two junked cars to every residence."

So now when you stand where the old fishermen did, you'll see barges instead of basalt, sailboarders instead of dip-netters, and tourists needing a restroom instead of traders looking for a deal. It's a strip of green with patches of trees, surrounded by the rumble and whine of traffic, the scrape of backhoes, the smell of slack water, and the wash of that water along a pebbled spot of shore with Coke cans and potato chips scattered among the blackberry tangles that grow from backwater seeps. Except for the wrinkled bark of the cottonwoods and the crinkle of feet scuffing leaves, it's the edge of a world gone slack, and smooth, and still, the roil of its river buried beneath the sluggish surface.

"Celilo Park, on Lake Celilo, is operated by the Corps," says the U.S. Army Corps of Engineers, "and has facilities for picnicking, fishing, swimming and boat launching." But unless you're looking for it, you won't find anything that tells you what this place used to be.

So look for a graffiti-scrawled restroom built of cinder block and painted the color of an unripe pumpkin. Nearby, next to the dumpsters in the parking lot, stands the one sign that summarizes the history of this place—the falls, the dam, the drowning.

"The loss of [Celilo] Falls did not mean the loss of the Indian way of life," it says. And the word *not* is blotted out in a dripping smudge of black paint.

Christmas Valley

It's the home of a lost forest and a cracked ground, of lakes without water and sand dunes without ocean shores. And anyone who travels through this land of curiosities and contradictions in central Oregon's Christmas Valley will find a story of how the earth has changed since the time of erupting volcanoes.

Northern Lake County is a land of hayfields and sage flats, where the pumps and pipes of circle irrigation systems struggle to hold back the desert. Past the pavement, rutted roads and swirling dust mark the entrance into the backcountry of the Christmas Valley basin and hills. Along these backroads that stretch east and north from the town of Christmas Valley, you'll find at least four chapters of a unique history.

Fossil Lake

The journey begins some 16 miles northeast of town in an area that today is dry, dusty desert. But 10,000 years ago, Fossil Lake covered the entire basin now holding both Fort Rock and Christmas Valley. In those days, the lake's shores were home to mammoths, camels and flamingos; its waters, to fish.

The fossils found in this area now—some dating back two million years—are rare, the Bureau of Land Management (BLM) says, because they come from "small mammals not normally found in such volume and variety."

Although collecting fossils is against Federal law, you can still walk within the fenced area enclosing some 6,500 acres of the old lake. But be warned, a restricted budget has resulted in spotty maintenance, so this area may be poorly marked even though it's adjacent to the road.

Sand Dunes

When Mount Mazama erupted over 7,000 years ago, some of its ash and pumice blew into the Christmas Valley basin. The result is a rolling stretch of wind-blown sand that covers 16,000 acres and reaches 60 feet in height. The BLM calls it "the largest inland moving sand dune system in the Pacific Northwest."

The Christmas Valley Chamber of Commerce, however, advertises it as "some of the best ATV (All Terrain Vehicle) riding in central Oregon." As a result, you'll find the whining motors and spinning tires of dune buggies and motorcycles almost everywhere along this stretch of road.

"This area sees only about 8,000 visitors per year," says a man familiar with the area. "But it seems like every one of them is driving an off-road vehicle."

Lost Forest

With the sand humped to the south and the sagebrush everywhere else, the road gets rougher as you travel deeper into the desert, until in the distance emerges a line of trees, a forest rising from the desert, its pines standing above the sage. This is the beginning of the Lost Forest.

Two sentry pines mark the entrance to this forest where ponderosa pines—along with the neighboring juniper, sagebrush, and bitterbrush—make up almost 6,000 acres of the 9,000 acre complex known as the Lost Forest Research Natural Area, which was established in 1972.

Actually, the forest here isn't so much lost as misplaced, for it stands in the middle of a desert where pine trees are supposed to die instead of thrive. Located 40 miles from the nearest pine forest neighbor in a land where summer temperatures can exceed 100 degrees, these pines receive less than ten inches of the minimum 14 inches of precipitation they require in a year. As a result, don't expect the towering, orange-bellied pines so common through much of central Oregon.

"The trees aren't that spectacular until you compare it to the desert you've been driving through," says a woman along the road with her Labrador retriever. "In that way, the forest is a curiosity."

It's also durable. By the first decade of the twentieth century, more than 100 homesteads in the area depended on the Lost Forest pines for building, fencing, and heating. Even though droughts drove out most of the homesteaders by the 1920s, the post World War II years saw the coming of timber companies that began once again to log the forest.

For more than 25 years, however, Lost Forest's designation as a Research Natural Area has stopped logging and protected the trees, and the presence of young pines means the forest is regenerating itself, providing a home to jackrabbits, mule deer, pronghorns, and even elk.

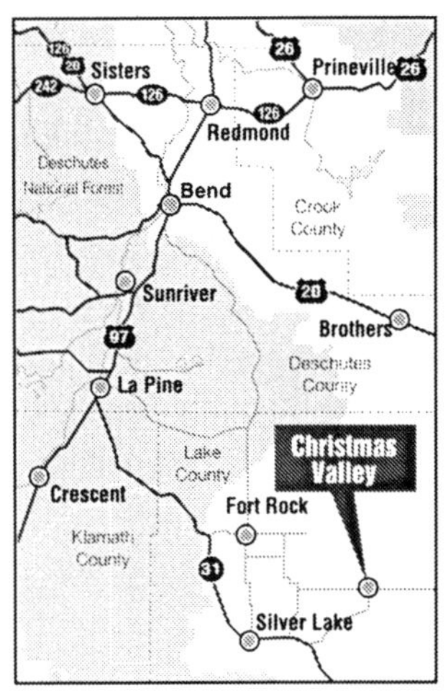

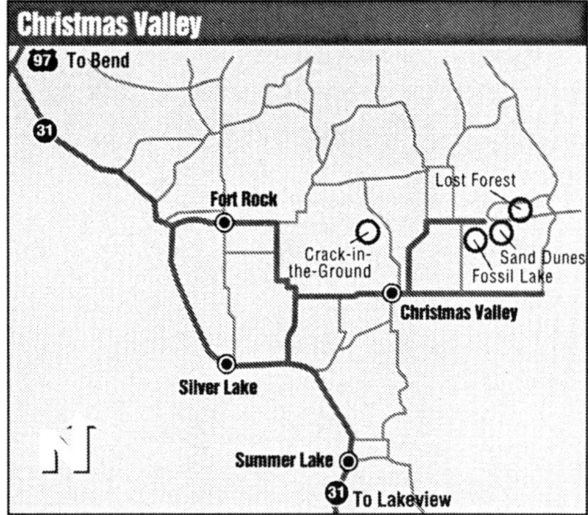

Where to Go

•Fossil Lake, Sand Dunes, Lost Forest, and Crack in the Ground all lie northeast of the town of Christmas Valley and are accessibly by county roads.

What to Expect

•None of the backroads in this area are regularly maintained, and many are not recommended for passenger cars. Expect lots of rocks and dust but few signs.

Things to Know

•Christmas Valley is part of the BLM's Christmas Valley Backcountry Byway, a 102-mile route along both gravel and paved roads.

Who to Contact

•For more information, contact the BLM's Lakeview office at 541-947-2177.

Crack in the Ground

North of the town of Christmas Valley, a washboard road divides the land—sage on one side, hay on the other, with quail and jackrabbits swapping sides as they see fit. In the distance, a juniper-spotted rim marks the climb out of the basin and the way into volcanic rubble still watched over by the four cinder cones that created it.

If you make the drive when the morning is bright and clean, the early chill carries the scent of juniper and sage, the whistle and chirp of birds. At the top of the rim, the road grows smoother, the sky bluer as you wind past bluebirds and robins that dip and flutter from roadside fence posts and juniper trees, seemingly leading you to the parking area that marks the entry to Crack In The Ground.

From here, a quarter-mile walk takes you to a jumble of rocks with the smell of a cellar. This is the Crack, created over 1,100 years ago with the eruption of the four craters to the north. When the ooze and spew of lava released enough pressure underground to make a nearby chunk of land collapse, it left an open fissure approximately two miles long and as much as 70 feet deep. Through this fissure now runs a 400 yard trail that shows you what happens when the earth cracks.

Down into the shadows the trail descends, past rocks and through crevices that can wedge you as tight as an Edgar Allan Poe crypt. High on the wall, the ledges grow shrubs, but down near the trail, where the sun only blinks at the crevice, wilted grass and scrawny junipers struggle through another season.

"It feels so prehistoric," says a woman along the trail with her Labrador retriever (same woman, same dog as were wandering the Lost Forest). "You almost expect to see Raquel Welch dressed in a fur bikini."

Although you won't see Raquel as you walk the trail and scramble over its boulders, you will see signs of wildlife (deer droppings) as well as modern life (graffiti scrawls and beer cans). Above you, rocks that have toppled from the walls over the last ten centuries squeeze themselves into a stony ceiling.

If, however, you prefer rocks beneath your feet instead of over your head, you'll be happy to know that the trail plunges and rises, plunges and rises, so whenever you pop into the open you can stay on top, exploring the Crack from ground level, walking the makeshift trails that line the edges of the fissure.

And here in the daylight of the old lake's basin, you'll find always the sound of birds, always the scent of sage, always the sense of a land's history even older than the fossils, the forests, and the fissures it holds.

Collier State Park

Once upon a time in Oregon, the forests were full of timber beasts, river pigs, and bullwhackers. And they weren't alone. They slept beside flume herders and skid greasers, shared their meals with pond monkeys and donkey punchers. Yes, the woods was quite a place in the early days of logging.

But the logger's world has always been a place of rapid and dramatic changes, from snorting oxen to clattering engines, from misery whips to power saws. Because of the speed of this metamorphosis, one place in southern Oregon has taken on the job of preserving the history of logging—Collier State Memorial Park.

Located along the Williamson River some 30 miles south of Klamath Falls, the park consists of more than 800 acres of campgrounds, picnic areas, and hiking trails. Yet it is the outdoor logging museum that attracts the most attention.

The museum had its start in 1946, when Alfred and Andrew Collier of Klamath Falls donated the park site to the state as a memorial to their parents. Two years later, in an effort to show the evolution of logging from earliest days to modern times, the brothers donated a collection of antique equipment to the fledgling park.

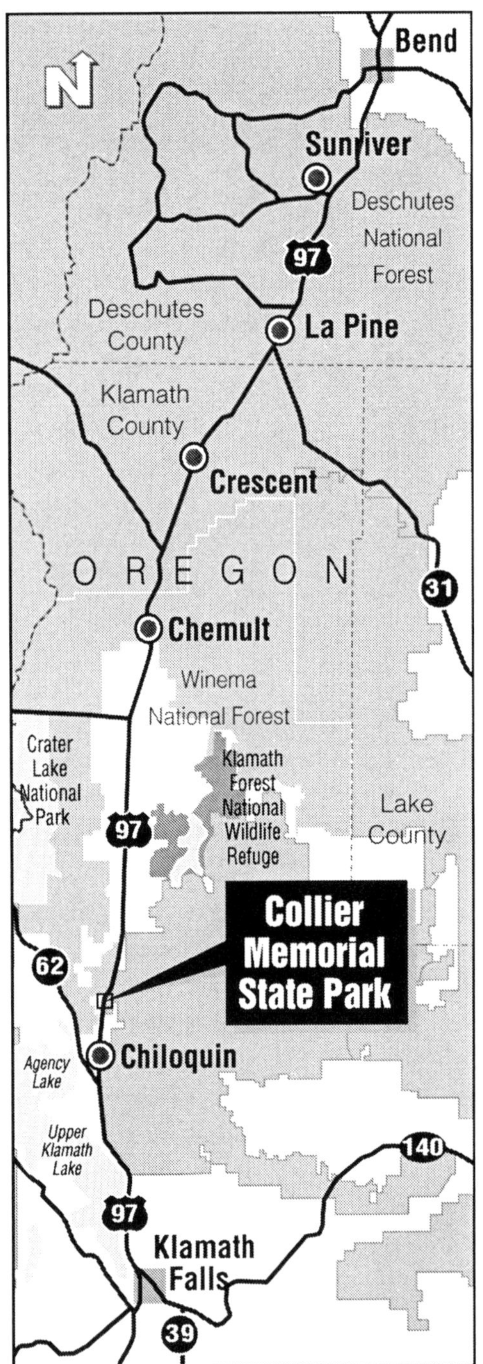

That collection has since grown into what some say is the largest and finest exhibit of pioneer logging equipment in the nation. Scattered across the museum grounds are sheds holding the tools, machines, and gear that preserve the memory of logging's past, the record of how loggers built the roads, cut the trees, and hauled the logs.

If you walk the trail connecting these sheds, you'll wander through a compact history of the men and machines who played the starring roles in one of Oregon's most important industries.

Through the early years of logging, the basic jobs of the timber beasts, the men working in the woods, remained the same. Using axes, wedges, and crosscut saws, fallers cut the trees and buckers severed them into chunks. Then the bullwhackers, the teamsters driving the oxen, hooked their yoked teams to the logs and led them out along skid roads, which skid greasers had swabbed with whale oil, rancid butter, or animal fat. The roads led either to a river (where men called river pigs started a river drive), to a flume (where flume herders kept the logs moving through the chute) or to a mill (where pond monkeys steered the logs from the water and to the saws).

Year after year, loggers used the same tools and followed the same routine. This constancy is evident as you begin your stroll along the museum's trail, for among the first displays is that of an 1860s blacksmith's shop. On exhibit here are reminders of the human and animal muscle used in logging's early days—the forge, anvil, and bellows used for making and repairing tools, as well as the harnesses, yokes, and shoes used for working the oxen. Nearby are horse-powered saws, wagons, and skids.

But just as that kind of power began to evolve into new forms in the 1880s, so do the museum's exhibits begin to focus on tracing the fuel systems that revolutionized the industry. The first of these revolutions came on the day when steam replaced oxen. When that happened, the steam donkey became a steam-snorting, winch-cranking beast of the woods.

Standing on wooden skids and powered by a wood-burning boiler and a one-cylinder engine, the steam donkey earned its

Where to Go

•The park is located on Highway 97, 107 miles south of Bend and 30 miles north of Klamath Falls.

When to Go

•The logging museum is open daily from dawn till dusk, and the day-use area is open year-round.

What to Expect

•Trail guides are available at the museum's gift shop and information center.

Things to Know

•Near the museum's parking area is a section of what was once the largest fir tree in Oregon. More than 200 feet tall and almost 16 feet in diameter, it was 702 years old when a 1962 storm knocked it down near Seaside.

Who to Contact

•For more information, call 541-783-2471.

name because some loggers thought it looked too puny for its power to be rated in horsepower. They were wrong.

Before long, winches and cables replaced yokes and rope, and donkey punchers (the machines' engineers) replaced bull-whackers. This caused such deep lament among some of the old timers that one of them wrote a bunkhouse poem about it, part of which goes like this:

But now, alas, my days are past;
there's no job for me here.
My bulls are killed and my place is filled
by a donkey engineer.

When you first see a steam donkey at the museum, you might wonder how such a little fellow could cause so much ruckus. That's what a turn-of-the-century writer thought before he saw one in action, skidding logs in the western Cascades.

"It is an awesome sight," he wrote, "to see a log six feet through and 40 feet long bounding toward you as if the devil were on it, breaking off some trees as if they were twigs, leaping over obstacles, gouging a way for itself."

Just as steam powered the donkeys that skidded the logs out of the woods, it fueled the tractors and locomotives that hauled them to the mills, and generated the electricity that ran the mill's saws. The grounds of the museum are covered with such machines, which served as the source of power for the timber industry until the 1920s. Then it was steam's turn to be replaced.

When the gasoline-fueled Caterpillar replaced the steam donkey in the 1920s, it marked the beginning of modern logging. Then in the 1930s, diesel replaced gasoline; and in the 1940s, trucks replaced trains and power saws replaced the crosscut.

Yet even the power saw wasn't the end of logging's evolution, for one of the museum's most modern pieces of equipment is the computer-operated Beloit Tree Harvestor. This machine cuts the tree, limbs it, and then stacks it for loading. It's so efficient and fast that it takes the place of an entire logging crew from the days of the steam donkey. Maybe that's why it costs a million dollars.

Even though this machine comes near the end of the trail of logging history, an adjacent section shifts you back a hundred years—the Pioneer Village, which consists of a dozen cabins brought in from different parts of southern Oregon. Just as the displays of the logging museum show you how people worked in the last century, the cabins in the Pioneer Village show you how they lived.

The cabins, which date from the 1870s to the 1890s, are built mostly from logs that are hewn, notched, and chinked. They include a general store and a trapper's cabin, a smokehouse and a doctor's office, a barn and a privy (which a sign explains served "one of mankind's most basic needs"). Their floors are dirt or wood, their windows shuttered or glassed; inside are stoves and skillets, boots and buckets, coffee pots and cooking utensils—all the stuff of life in a home a century ago.

And outside those homes were the forests, a world where men breathed sawdust and machines bellowed steam, in a time when the woods belonged to the timber beasts.

Fort Dalles

In the days when the Oregon country reached from the Pacific to the Rockies, a single army post on the Columbia River watched over it—Fort Dalles. From here, soldiers patrolled wagon roads and protected gold miners, helped emigrants and fought Indians. Although the years have whittled away at this once isolated guardian of pioneers, enough is left give you a look at what life was like in frontier Oregon.

"It's a glimpse into everyday life back then—its struggles and triumphs," says a woman visiting the fort. "But it's not organized, not sequential. And that's part of its charm."

Indeed, the buildings and grounds of the museum contain not only the gear of pioneer life, but also some of its clutter. As one visitor says, "They don't spoon feed history to you here. You have to leaf through books and peek into corners."

When you do, you'll find pieces of a story that, like so many other chapters in Oregon history, begin with the entrance of the first missionaries. After starting life as a Methodist mission in 1838, the post became a resting place for Oregon Trail emigrants before they tackled the rapids of the Columbia River or the slopes of Mount Hood.

But then the war that followed the 1847 Whitman Massacre turned the mission buildings into an army post—Camp Drum, a collection of dirt-floored buildings that housed a few dozen men. "A most desolate place," wrote a lieutenant stationed there, "with nothing to recommend it except wolves, coyotes, rattlesnakes and skunks."

Miserable as it was, the fort and its ten square miles of ground stood as the only army post between Fort Vancouver to the west, located near the confluence of the Willamette and Columbia rivers; and Fort Laramie to the east, situated at about the halfway point of the Oregon Trail, in what is today Wyoming. For the most part, it was a land that had yet to see a farm or a fence.

"If any country in the world has ever merited the title of Indian country," wrote the fort's commander, "this is it."

In the 1850s, however, gold strikes and wagon trains pulled more whites into this country, and that brought more soldiers to the fort as a means of maintaining peace. The fort's new importance as a regimental headquarters and supply depot created dramatic changes.

According to an officer stationed there in 1855, Fort Dalles was located in a "dreary, isolated spot...destitute of all that makes life agreeable." Yet only three years later, Salem's *Oregon Statesman* reported that "The buildings, and all the improvements are of the best and most substantial character, and the garrison is said to be the most comfortable one on the Pacific."

What happened in those three years? Two men arrived at Fort Dalles—Captain Thomas Jordan, the post's new quartermaster, who had plans for rebuilding the fort, and Louis Scholl, the captain's civilian clerk and a skilled architect, who began designing quarters "for taste superior to those we have seen at any other post."

They built this new fort above the flood plain and near a spring, with a view of the Columbia River and looking squarely into the face of Mount Adams. "The fort's parade ground is the grade school's playground," says the museum's Dottie Guth. She points down the hill to the nearby school. "And the school's flag pole is exactly where the fort's was."

By using local timber, stone, and labor—over 200 civilians earned total wages of over $14,000 per month—Jordan and Scholl soon accomplished their goal. The most impressive building was Colonel George Wright's house, which cost $22,000 to build in 1856. (In comparison, the wages of the carpenters, masons, and blacksmiths who built it averaged approximately five dollars a

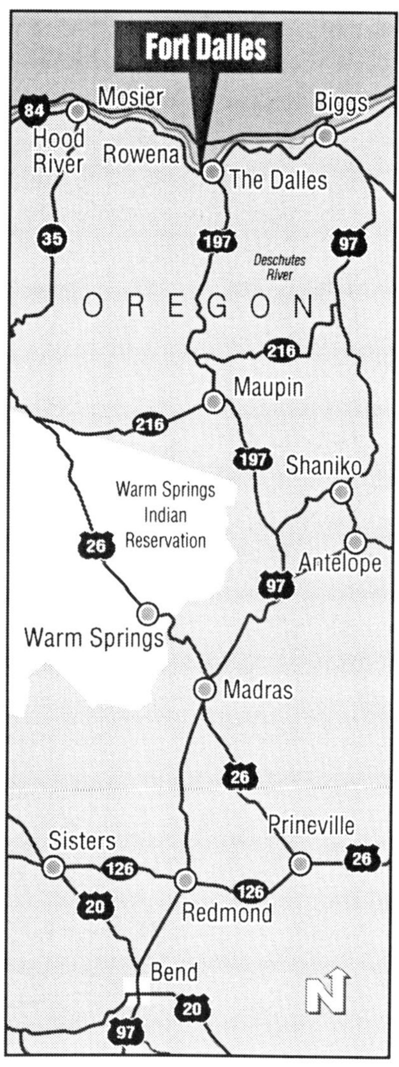

day.) It was, according to Scholl, "the finest house in all Oregon."

Today, however, only a stone memorial and a grove of pine trees mark its location. The home, like many of the other buildings, fell victim to fire between 1865 and 1867. "Those fires," Guth says, "were probably caused by bad mortar in the chimneys."

After the post was abandoned as an active military fort in 1867, almost four decades of weather and scavengers tore away at what was left. By the time a group of local women rescued it at the turn of the century, only two of the original buildings remained, the gardener's cottage and the surgeon's quarters.

In 1905 the surgeon's quarters—described at the time as "one of the loveliest little buildings in the state"—experienced a transformation, first undergoing repair and then opening as a historical museum. That inauguration as a storehouse of memorabilia more than 90 years ago makes Fort Dalles one of Oregon's oldest museums.

Standing now at the hub of the museum's complex and holding the core of its collection, this remnant of the old fort is testimony to the elegance of nineteenth-century architecture (its original construction cost was just under $5,000), to the durability of its wood and stone (except for the floor and roof, the building is the 1856 original), and to the labor and diligence of the volunteers who maintain it. As one visitor says, "The people who run this place really seem to care."

That care is evident throughout the building's rooms, where cases and cupboards and racks display the history of both the region and the fort. Indian artifacts and pioneer relics, army equipment and household furnishings, photographs of the times and drawings of the buildings—these things and much more occupy the rooms where the post's surgeon once worked.

"Within the building, and within the rooms within the building, there are surprises," says a visitor. "It's an exercise in discovery."

A short stroll across the grounds leads you to other discoveries. One building, set up like a giant garage, displays a collection of historical vehicles, ranging from stagecoaches and surreys to an 1870s hearse and an 1890s bicycle; another, across the road, is the Anderson House and its nearby barn, remarkable examples of hand-hewn craftsmanship from the turn of the century.

"Mr. Anderson was a dry land wheat farmer who built his barn before he built his house," Guth says. "But when the house was done, Mrs. Anderson was proud because she had a two-seat privy."

That pride is understandable. Because the settlements in this region had their beginnings in lonely missions and remote outposts, those who built their homes and raised their families near old Fort Dalles might have seen the two-seater as a symbol of their small victory over the frontier, as another step toward civilization.

Where to Go

- From Interstate 84, take Exit 85 at The Dalles and then follow the signs.

When to Go

- The fort is open year-round. Call for days and times.

Things to Know

- Camp Drum—and later Fort Drum—was named for Captain Simon H. Drum, who in the fall of 1850 helped emigrants who "had consumed their last biscuit, and had not as much as a bacon rine (sic) to grease their wagons, for some three weeks or a month."
- The fort never had a stockade.

Who to Contact

- For more information, call the fort at 541-296-4547.

Fort Rock

If you drive the lonely roads into the High Lava Plains of south-central Oregon, you'll find jackrabbits skittering their zig-zag way across a lake bottom. Of course, the lake's water is gone, as are the camels, mammoths and bison that once grazed along its shore, and the flamingos that once waded through its shallows. But what's left behind is one of the nation's most important archaeological sites—Fort Rock.

Located off Highway 31 between Bend and Lakeview, Fort Rock—a solitary citadel of volcanic rock looming above the desert's sagebrush and alkali—has been a landmark for as long as people have lived in this area. Now a state park, this rock gives you the chance to take a short walk through a long history. Yet to understand how it got here and what it means, we have to go back to its beginning, 100,000 years ago.

In that long-ago time, a vast lake filled the Fort Rock basin, stretching east to Christmas Valley and south to Silver Lake, and reaching a depth of almost 200 feet. Beneath the surface, however, the earth was restless. Magma-molten rock was busily squeezing its way upward.

On its journey toward daylight, however, this magma pushed itself into the mud and ooze of the lake bottom. Heat and water collided into steam. The steam triggered an eruption. Time after time, lava and mud exploded into the air, and the red-hot geyser of gooey ash plopped down around the vent in layers, hardened into rock, and formed a ring around the crater. The result was a circular island anchored in the lake—Fort Rock.

Although this island was originally 400 feet tall and more than a mile wide, the lake's waves began nibbling away at the rock, finally gnawing a hole in its south side. This is probably the way the area's first people found the island when they arrived near the end of the last Ice Age, more than 10,000 years ago. And it is this human history that makes Fort Rock so special.

Not long ago, archaeologists believed the first humans made their way to the Pacific Northwest only a few thousand years ago. But then in 1938, Luther S. Cressman, a professor at the University of Oregon, began excavating a cave near Fort Rock.

"Dust devils swirled across miles of shimmering space in the dancing heat mirage," Cressman wrote. "The accumulated refuse of centuries, rodent droppings, dust, ash, all had a characteristic stench that clung to our nostrils as did the dust to our sweaty bodies."

But Cressman and his students kept digging, and what they found lying beneath a layer of volcanic ash rippled through the worlds of archeology and anthropology. "We...came upon a sandal...unlike any we had ever found," Cressman wrote.

It was unlike what *anyone* had ever found before in North America, and they found 75 pairs of them, all woven from sagebrush bark. What set these sandals apart was their age, more than 9,000 years old. And the people who wore them lived in a much different world.

"The wearers of these sandals did not look out on swirling dust devils or miles of alkali and sand flats as we did that hot August day," Cressman wrote, "but on a great lake with wavelets lapping against a beach below the cave."

In their wave-cut caves, these ancient Oregonians slept on beds of grass and burned sagebrush for firewood. Nearby grazed the horses, camels, mammoths and bisons they hunted with spears and atlatls and butchered with obsidian knives.

Even as the lake began shrinking and the sagebrush expanding under a drying climate, these people made their homes in the Fort Rock basin. And because it's been a state park since 1962, you

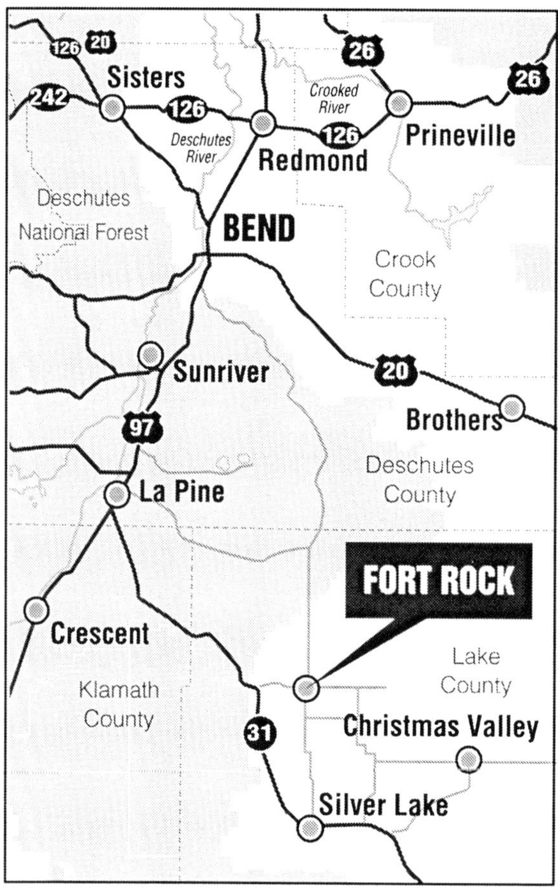

are now welcome to take a stroll through the place those people called home a hundred centuries ago.

The parking and picnic area for the park is located less than two miles from the town of Fort Rock. (Because the town, the valley, and the cave, as well as the rock, all share the Fort Rock name it sometimes creates confusion.)

From here a series of paths and a couple of roads wander through the formation. The most obvious trail begins on asphalt just past the information kiosk and leads to the few trailside interpretive signs.

Up the slope is one of the most dramatic examples of the forces that shaped the rock, for you can see clearly where the lake's waves carved into the sides a series of terraces that were once beaches along the shoreline. Past here, the trail follows a rough loop of approximately a mile around the inside perimeter of the formation.

Sometimes compared to a ruined castle, a huge horseshoe, or even "a giant doughnut with most of one side munched off," Fort Rock's more than 300-foot high presence on the flat basin floor is imposing. But that impression grows even stronger up close.

"It's impressive from a distance," says a woman along the trail, "but almost overwhelming when you're close to it."

Once inside you'll find another change as waist-high bunchgrass and knee-high sage, which rustle with the hop of cottontail rabbits or the wriggle of short-horned lizards, soften the honey-combed rock walls that slope up from the old vent and stack up against the sky in jagged peaks and pockets. Even though the main trail follows the base of the rim, spur trails lead to the ridges, so you can circle the formation at the level you want.

"Not often do you get to walk in 10,000 years old footsteps," says a man along one of the trails.

"Actually, you do," his wife says. "It's just that here you're so conscious of it."

Along this trail, you're also aware of the land the way it was long ago, for when the sun shines on the basin and heat shimmers from its floor, waves still roll across the lake bed and ripple toward its shore.

Where to Go

- The Fort Rock turnoff is approximately 30 miles southeast of La Pine on Highway 31.
- Nearby attractions include Hole-in-the-Ground and Big Hole, mile-wide craters created by steam explosions.

What to Expect

- You'll find drinking water and restrooms at the Fort Rock parking area.

Things to Know

- The horse, camel, and mammoth became extinct in the New World approximately 7,500 years ago. This coincides with the drying of the ancient lakes.
- Fort Rock (the rock) and the surrounding land were donated to the state by area rancher Reub Long. Fort Rock (the cave) was made a National Historic Landmark in 1963.
- Luther S. Cressman died in 1994 at the age of 96.

Painted Hills

Gerard Manley Hopkins, a nineteenth-century English poet, never saw the Painted Hills of central Oregon. But he wrote about them anyway:

Glory be to God for dappled things—
For skies of couple-color as a brinded cow;
For rose-moles all in stipple upon trout that swim;
Fresh-firecoal chestnut-falls; finches' wings;
Landscape plotted and pierced—fold, fallow, and plow...

These lines from a Hopkins' poem—which celebrates the beauty of a world clouded and rounded, patched and shaded, streaked, speckled, and flecked—describe the Painted Hills Unit, a Wheeler County segment of the John Day Fossil Beds National Monument. Yet these color-layered hills seem to attract more people interested in geology and paleontology than they are in poetry, for the land tells a long and vital story of life on Earth. To help you experience both the art and the science of the place, four trails lead you through some of its major parts.

The best introduction to the area probably comes from the Overlook Trail, a half mile gravel path that stretches along a gentle ridge and ends with a view of distance and depth. From here you'll see the earth lying in rolls and folds, in wrinkles and creases, and stroked with swatches of grass and sage and juniper. This view looks like a topographical map come alive, the layers running in ripples of red and green and brown, with the white streaks of deer-tracked trails etching their flanks.

Where did the Painted Hills get their color? Once upon a time, over 30 million years ago, a chain of volcanoes stood where the Cascade Mountains would one day rise. These volcanoes began erupting, belching clouds of fiery spew, and layer by layer the ash and the pumice buried the land.

As millennia passed, lava flooded over this same area, cooling into a rock-cap layer that covered the ash beds. Then along came wind and water, which began carving away at the hills, scraping away the layers, sculpting the land into gentle curves. A push here, and the surface lifted; a pull there and the layers shifted.

What shows now, after millions of years of the soils and minerals squeezing and mixing together, are the colors of those layers—red, blue, green, gray, and yellow. "This is a gently contoured piece of geologic violence," the interpretive sign tells you.

But this is more than a nice phrase, for if you line up the hillside colors—for instance, the red on a crest with the red on a slope—you'll see how the earth heaved and rose and settled. Across a sunrise sky, when the sun lifts from behind Sutter Mountain, the streaks of red clouds seem to mirror the ground.

For an aerial view of the same landscape, hike the Carroll Rim Trail, which shares the road junction with the Overlook Trail. This trail climbs three quarters of a mile toward the eastern sky and puts you near the rimrocked top of the Fossil Bed world. Along the way you'll find squadrons of ravens winging above, rolls of earth lying below in humped ridges to the south.

Near the summit of the trail is a ridgetop saddle that curls behind Carroll Rim. At the far downhill end of a sweeping slope of bunchgrass and sagebrush, farm fields hayed and plowed lie in the distance. On top of the rim is silence and sun and a bench where you can sit and listen for the chuckles of chukars, or watch for the swoop of golden eagles or prairie falcons.

In contrast to the steep ascent to Carroll Rim, the trail around Painted Cove, located only a mile down the road, is a flat loop that gives you a close-up view of what happened to that 30 million year old volcanic ash. A quarter-mile stroll takes you past 11 stops, each of which offers you a lesson in geology—why the hills have the texture of popcorn (the clay expands when it absorbs water, then cracks when it dries), why they change colors (a wet surface seals and reflects light, and a dry surface contracts and diffuses light), and why they're bare of plants (water and roots can penetrate only a few inches into the hillsides).

While Painted Cover offers lessons in geology, the quarter-mile Leaf Hill Trail—only another mile down the road—gives instruction in botany. At the time those ancient volcanoes began belching their ash, this was a land of large tortoises and small horses, of flesh-eating dogs and leaf-eating oreodonts. It was also a land of hardwood forests. Oak, maple, alder, and beech grew here.

Of course, the leaves, twigs and fruits from this forest fell to the ground and washed into nearby creeks and ponds. But when the volcanoes erupted, their ash buried this forest debris in muddy stream bottoms.

Now when today's streams cut into the shale, the shale splits, and leaf fossils appear. This extraordinary deposit of fossilized leaves tells us what life was like here ages ago. "Much of what is now known about the ancient forests once growing in eastern Oregon was learned at this site," says thc National Park Service.

But while the land's fossils are buried, its poetry wavers across its surface and hovers in the air. As Mr. Hopkins put it in a line from a different poem: "It will flame out, like shining from shook foil..." This makes it easy to find for anybody looking for the poetry that echoes from a special place.

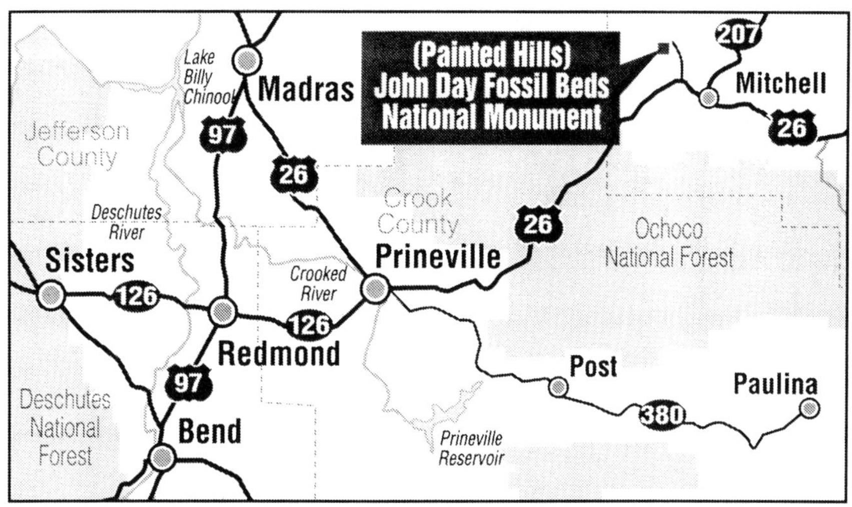

Where to Go

•On Highway 26 approximately six miles west of Mitchell, look for the Painted Hills sign between mileposts 62 and 63.

When to Go

•Most of the park's 130,000 annual visitors come through in July and August; the fewest, in January.

What to Expect

•HIKING IS PERMITTED ON ESTABLISHED TRAILS ONLY! Please. The land is so very fragile.

Things to Know

•The three units of the John Day Fossil Beds consist of 14,000 total acres—almost 22 square miles.

•The poems of Gerard Manley Hopkins were not published until 1918, almost 30 years after his death.

Who to Contact

•For more information, call the park's Painted Hills office at 541-462-3961.

Steins Pillar

The story begins long, long ago when the Blue Mountains formed the seashore of what is now Oregon. Back then, the Ochoco

Mountains were a string of coastal volcanoes waiting to erupt. When they did, lava and ash buried the nearby valleys and hills.

Now push the fast-forward button on Earth history and jump ahead 44 million years to the Mill Creek Valley of central Oregon. Rain, wind, and frost have gnawed away at the valley's tuff—volcanic ash compacted into rock—for so long that only the plugs of a few eroded volcanoes remain. Perhaps the most dramatic, even beautiful, of these is Steins Pillar, a spire 350 feet high and 120 feet wide, shaped like a craggy finger poking out of the hillside and pointing at the sky.

Located in the Ochoco National Forest on the edge of the Mill Creek Wilderness, the trail to Steins Pillar is an example of how a non-wilderness trail can lead to a backcountry experience complete with ancient forests and mountain views. (The pillar is named for Major Enoch Steen, who led an 1860 army expedition through the area in search of a wagon route between northwest and southeast Oregon; according to the U.S. Forest Service, Steins Pillar "was misspelled so often that the incorrect version became official.")

The journey begins approximately 10 miles east of Prineville, where you turn off Highway 26 and onto Forest Service Road 33 (also called Mill Creek Road). From here the road curves through a narrow, pine-lined valley that holds a winding, gravelly stream. The pavement ends at about the five mile mark, and the side road splitting off to the trailhead is about a mile and a half beyond.

Instead of turning at the junction, however, travel another mile and a half to the viewpoint. This will let you see the pillar from the sweep of valley it seems to rule, as well as give you the geological explanation of the pillar's origins.

Once you backtrack to the junction, drive across the Mill Creek bridge and head uphill on a steep climb past orange-barked, old-growth ponderosa pine trees. Although you won't find a sign marking the trailhead, a well-used turnaround at about the two-mile mark shows you the trail's beginning; if you should miss it, a nearby roadblock stops you from going too far.

The hike begins on a downhill slope that leads across a stream and through a stand of pines growing round and smooth and tall in the needle-filtered sunlight. On a cool day, the shade in this swale can be icy, but a few short, steep switchbacks soon lead you to a hilltop route that stretches along the spine of the ridge and into the sunlight.

Above you are hawks gliding on the thermals that sweep up the hillsides; across from you, slopes pleated with draws and shaggy with pines. And above it all, the blue-hazed southwest horizon seems to prop up the distant white peaks of the Three Sisters.

As the path leads down onto the slope, however, this view begins blending into the groves of mountain mahogany that stand twisted along the hillside, and the boulders of granite and basalt that lay tumbled among the juniper trees.

Before long the trail bends around the slope and into a draw, where the day turns cool and moist, and the footprints of elk dimple the ground. In these sanctuaries of shade, you'll find breezes seeping through your clothes, moss carrying the scent of earth, and lichen beards dangling from pine limbs.

Because the trail alternates this way between sunny slopes and shady draws all along the hour-long walk to the pillar, the routine you follow goes like this: across the face of a slope, around to the head of a draw, then out onto the face of a slope—sun and shade, warm and cool, open and tight.

This gives you a concise view of Mill Creek topography, which one authority says "preserves one of the Ochoco's few remaining climax forests of ponderosa pine and bunchgrass."

Even the forest's snags are imposing. "You have to plant your feet apart to keep your balance when you look up at them," says a woman along the trail with her Labrador retriever.

Soon after wandering past some of the largest of those snags, you'll find yourself coming to a bend in the trail—and there it is. Steins Pillar. More than 40 million years old.

"I saw Eternity the other night," wrote seventeenth-century poet Henry Vaughan, "Like a great ring of pure and endless light..."

Yet if Vaughan had seen Steins Pillar, perhaps he would have compared what he saw to a towering red pinnacle of broken and craggy rock. For those who want to stare into the face of such an eternity, hike on down the switchbacks for another ten minutes, through storm wreckage and down log steps, and you'll find yourself at the base of the pillar, staring up at any combination of eyes and noses and chins you have time for.

Imaginary ears and hair, moles and freckles, pimples and scars—these mark the eons-old expressions of Steins Pillar. "Intimidating," is the way one hiker describes the view from the base.

But while your imagination can give the rock its face, it can't account for its age. "Where there is no where and no when," is the way German philosopher Arthur Schopenhauer described eternity. Well maybe, but at the end of the trail to Steins Pillar, you can get a pretty good idea about how a chunk of it looks.

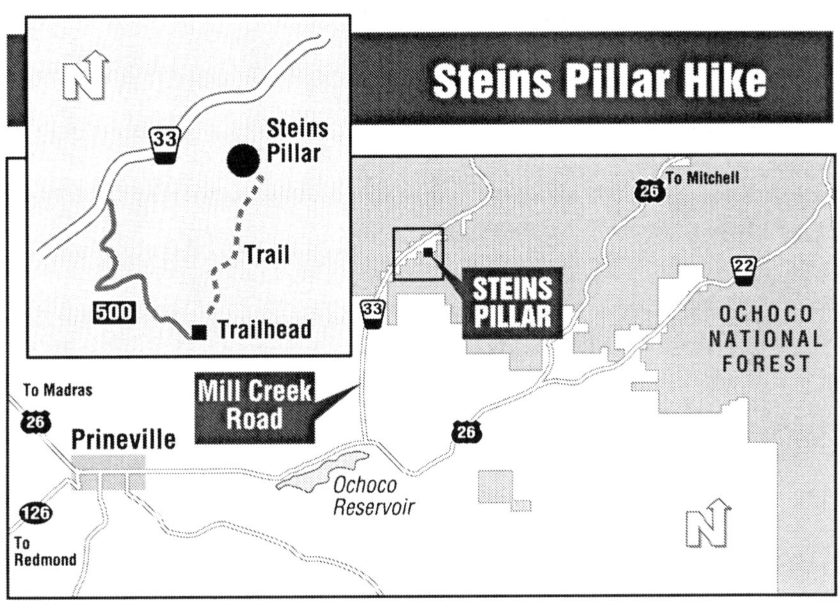

Where to Go

•Look for Mill Creek Road (U.S. Forest Service Road 33) near the east end of Ochoco Reservoir.

Things to Know

•The peak of Steins Pillar is 4,377 feet above sea level.

•Enoch Steen was a Kentuckian who died 20 years after his expedition through eastern Oregon. Steens Mountain in southeast Oregon, also named for the major, occasionally suffers from the same "Stein" misspelling.

•Rock climbers first scaled Steins Pillar in 1950.

Who to Contact

•For more information, call the USFS Prineville office at 541-447-6247.

Summer Lake

Almost 300 years ago, an Englishman who described himself as "a person of learning and piety" claimed that he had solved the mystery of where birds go when they migrate. They fly to the moon. He added, however, that the journey posed some problems, for after winging their way through space for 60 days to get there, the birds found no food. So they slept the winter away in hibernation. Hmm.

Even though we now have different ideas about the migration of birds, some of the mystery remains. For instance, one of the most important areas for migrating waterfowl in the Pacific Flyway is located in a desert basin of southeastern Oregon, a land of scarce rain, few streams, and salty water—Summer Lake. So critical is this land to ducks, geese, swans, cranes, and their assorted friends and relatives—250 species in all—that more than 50 years ago it was established as a place where wildlife could thrive in what the area's manager calls "an unspoiled, natural setting."

Lying at an elevation of over 4,200 feet in Lake County's high desert, the Summer Lake basin stretches out 20 miles in length and 10 miles in width, and holds approximately 60 square miles of alkaline water in a land-locked lake that barely rises above hipboot height. On the northern edge of the lake is the wildlife area—

almost 30 square miles of wetlands and uplands, lakes and marshes, streams and canals. And the birds love it.

"This is one of the best places in Oregon to view migrating waterfowl and other shore and waterbirds," says the Oregon Department of Fish and Wildlife (ODFW), which manages the wildlife area.

On their way south in the fall and north in the spring, migrating birds stop here by the thousands to rest, nest, feed, and breed. Although it may seem strange that the high desert can exert such a pull, the reason for the birds' behavior is found in the prehistoric past, when this area held a vast network of lakes and wetlands that was home to thousands of birds, especially geese and other waterfowl.

"Even when the climate changed and the great waters dried up and turned into desert basins, the geese kept coming, kept flying into the lakes that remained from the old seas," says the widely unacclaimed novel *The Roar of the Bear*. "They came out of the north by the thousands in the early fall, pulled by a genetic memory that led them into the Summer Lake Basin and onto the lake water covering the desert edge..."

Once a traditional summer home of the Northern Paiutes as well as a hunting and gathering place for the Modocs and Klamaths, Summer Lake became Oregon's first state-protected wildlife area in 1944. But it had started attracting tourists 101 years earlier. That's when Captain John C. Fremont and the U.S. Topographical Engineers, who were mapping a route between Oregon's Columbia River and California's Sacramento River, found themselves wallowing through three feet of snow on a 7,000-foot plateau, staring down into a sun-lit valley of grass and water far below. Fremont named the plateau Winter Ridge and the water Summer Lake, then promptly led his 27 troops down into the sunshine.

Three decades later, the area attracted a different group of people—its first settlers. After the first wagons creaked into the basin in 1871, enough others followed that within a few years almost 50 homesteads lay scattered across the basin. "Disappointment, hardships, sorrow and tragedy were the companions of most [settlers]," writes historian Teressa Foster, "but perseverance, endurance, bravery and determination were in the company also."

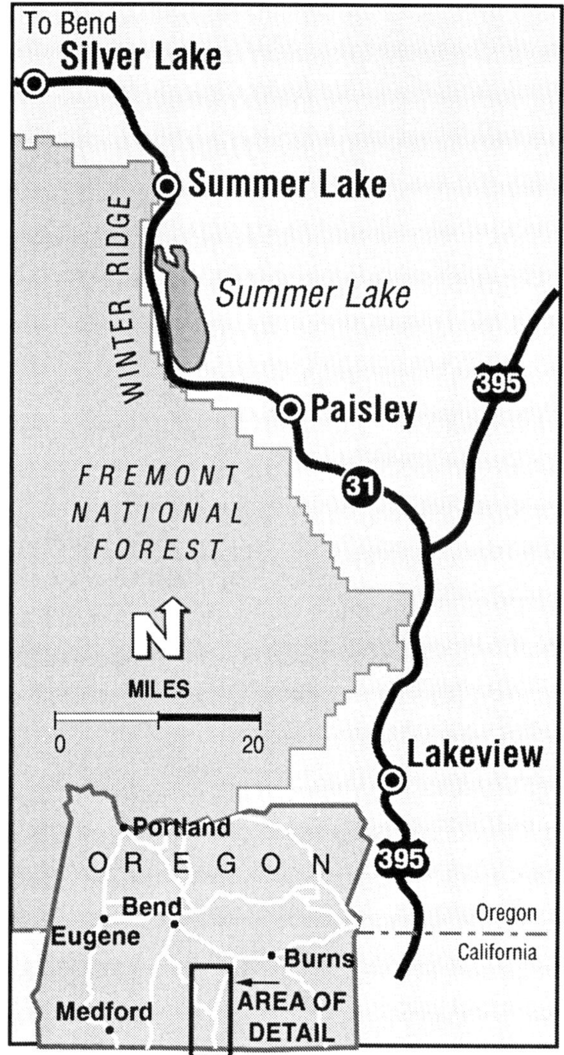

It seems that what separated a disappointed settler from a persevering one was water. Because the valley receives less than 10 inches of rain a year, and because the lake water is alkali, fresh water was precious to the homesteaders. The few who found it stayed; the many who didn't, left.

Signs of those homesteading days are still evident throughout the wildlife area, for it encompasses old farms, fields, barns, and school yards. Even the Ana River, whose five springs are the primary source of water for Summer Lake, is dammed into an irrigation reservoir, a project with roots running back more than 70 years, when two homesteading brothers first tried to water the basin's desert.

The ODFW folks also control the flow of water, though instead of dams they use dikes and canals to create wildlife habitat. This method of management also provides a road system that gives waterfowlers a route to hunting sites. The wildlife area is supported almost entirely by the sale of hunting licenses and stamps. It also provides other visitors a passageway into the heart of the marsh.

Lined with cattails and bulrushes, Russian olives and sagebrush, the Wildlife Viewing Loop runs for more than eight graveled miles along the dikes and through the wetlands.

"One way to travel the loop is by car," says a man touring the road on a bicycle. "But an even better way is this." He pats the seat of his bike. "This way you get a feel for the place." Then he blows on his hands and glances at the shadowy slope of Winter Ridge, which seems to be spitting snow. "Of course, sometimes that feeling can get a bit numb on a day like this."

Whether you drive or pedal, you'll find a special experience in traveling beneath a cloud-broken sky where hawks ride the air currents over ragged fields that waver gold with the wind-blown rustle of grass, over riffled water where coots scoot across the surface and ducks dabble beneath it. Because the refuge is at least a temporary home to more than two dozen species of ducks, the

Where to Go

•Summer Lake is located near Paisley on Highway 31, 100 miles southeast of Bend and 75 miles northwest of Lakeview.

When to Go

•Once hunting season begins in early October, much of the refuge road is closed until mid-January. For this reason, spring is probably the best time for viewing waterfowl, shorebirds, and songbirds.

What to Expect

•The wildlife area has four primitive camp sites.

Things to Know

•Kit Carson and Thomas Fitzpatrick, famous mountain men, served as scouts with Fremont's expedition.

•The Ana River was named in the 1890s for Ana Byars, the daughter of a Summer Lake surveyor.

Who to Contact

•For more information, contact the Wildlife Area at 541-943-3152.

canals sometimes seem to spout skyward on the wings of mallards, widgeons, gadwalls, pintails, or buffleheads.

And should you find yourself here during the spring or fall migration, you'll encounter one of the most extraordinary wildlife shows on the planet—the rise, the flight, and the voices of snow geese. Tens of thousands of snow geese. To watch them is to see the world erupt white beneath the tremor of flapping wings.

For years beyond understanding the flight of the snow geese has filled this valley; from the dawn of time their voices have sounded the return of spring. "It darn near stops your heart to hear them," the bicycle man says, adding that he thinks of the sound as the song of the geese. "And right now I figure I'm doing what people have been doing in this same place for thousands of years—waiting to hear that song again."

NORTHEAST

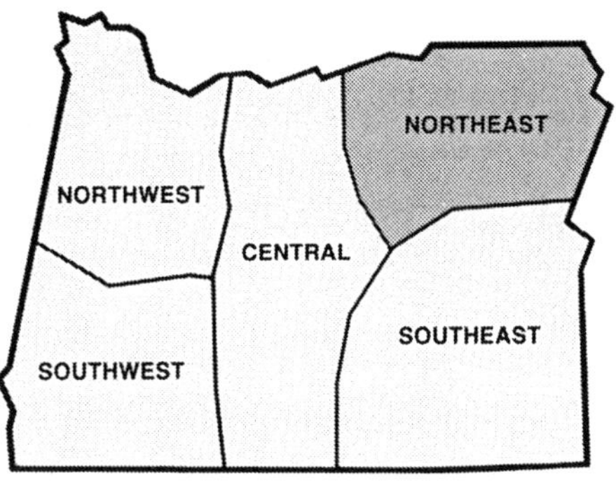

Blue Mountain Crossing

Elizabeth is a spry woman, especially for someone over 150 years old. Her eyes flash blue in the shadow of the emigrant wagon as she tells her stories of balking oxen and cursing men, of illness and accident and death along the Oregon Trail.

Well, okay—it's Elizabeth's great, great, great granddaughter who tells the stories, but its Elizabeth herself who wrote the script in the form of the diary she kept as she and her family made their way by wagon train toward the Willamette Valley. Today you can hear the words from that diary at Blue Mountain Crossing, an Oregon Trail interpretive park located in the mountains between Pendleton and La Grande.

What sets this park apart from other Oregon Trail sites are two special qualities. The first is the Trail itself, which the U.S. Forest Service calls, "Some of the best preserved traces of the Old Emigrant Road." Two connecting paths—"Discovery Loops"—lead you to them.

The longer of these is the Independence Loop. Along its three-quarter-mile length is a series of ten numbered posts, which help guide you through a brief history of the road that not only led pioneers, miners, and freighters over the Blue Mountains, but also served for decades as the primary connection between eastern and western Oregon.

The route curves down a gentle slope where you'll probably encounter chipmunks scampering across the fresh prints of deer or elk. You'll also find the tracks of freight wagons and stage coaches, for nearby lie the ruts where five old roads converge. These different roads resulted from rough terrain and road blocks.

"Our traviling through the timber was quite difficult," wrote an 1842 emigrant, "as the path wound back and forth and many logs lay across it."

When the path turns uphill toward the ridge, you'll climb out of the trees and up through wildflowers and sage to the ridge, where forested slopes drop steeply into the next drainage. According to the Forest Service, this hill looks much as it did in the time of the wagon trains, though it now grows more sagebrush and less bunch grass than it did prior to the westward migrations, when livestock began grazing the Blue Mountain region.

Because pioneers found their wagons tipped easily on side hills, they drove them straight up or down slopes like this one. The resulting ride could be a long, rough roll over the mountains. One emigrant described a section of trail as "...first up a long hill... then down a long ridge...then up another long ridge and down a steep hill...[then] onto the next ridge..."

On steep hills, wagons had to be "double teamed" by harnessing extra horses, mules, or cattle to them. "We went up one (hill) today and it took twenty-two head of cattle to haul up one wagon," wrote emigrant Elizabeth Wood, "and there was not much in the wagon either."

Along the ridge stand some of the last surviving witnesses to the great migrations of the last century—the pines and firs cut and scarred by the thousands of iron rims that once clunked against them. "I never saw as crooked a road in all my life," wrote one emigrant. "Some of the trees are rubbed one third the thickness through by the wagon hubs."

This road is still clearly marked, for the emigrants cleared rocks from the wagons' path and stacked them on the sides. Those stones too large to move they ran over, either crushing them into gravel or wearing them smooth. Either way, the labor and the erosion slowly opened the way for those who followed, increasing a wagon's eight mile day in the 1840s to a 20 mile day in the 1860s.

Although the wagon road continues across the Blues from here, the walking path turns aside when it connects with the Oregon City Loop, a quarter-mile trail that steers you toward the scent of a campfire. Follow it, and you'll find the second distinguishing quality of the park—the emigrant camp of Elizabeth and her husband, Andrew.

While Andrew splits the wood and tends the campfire, Elizabeth stands near the wagon in her soil stained bonnet and dress and describes their menu ("Everything is based on flour and salt"), their discoveries ("The Platte River is too thick to drink and too thin to plow"), and their difficulties ("Dysentery has plagued us the whole way"). But when they reach the Willamette Valley, she says, they will also reach the end of those difficulties—"No more plains to cross. No more burials to endure."

It is a history lesson with a human face. "But I learn more than the visitors do," says Andrew, who wears a wide brimmed hat and suspenders, wooden buttons on his trousers and mule ear pull-ons on his boots. "So many people who come here have their own Oregon Trail story to tell."

Those stories might be about why their ancestors made the journey, or how to grease an axle or hitch a team of oxen. Elizabeth's story, once she leaves her emigrant character, is that her great, great, great grandmother did not complete her journey, did not cross over these mountains. She's buried along the trail, somewhere nearby, "at the base of a yellow pine."

But until that end, Elizabeth's diary carries a message of hope typical of many emigrants. "Be of good cheer," she wrote. "We're going to see those trees of Oregon." One of those trees now marks her unfound grave in the Blue Mountains, near the crossing that carries the voices of pioneers.

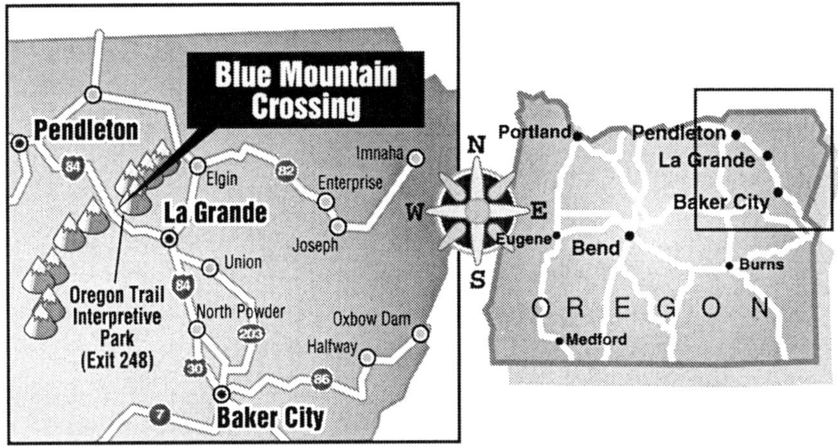

Where to Go

•From Interstate 84 take Exit 248. Follow the signs for three miles to the park.

When to Go

•Blue Mountain Crossing is open from 8 a.m. till 8 p.m. every day from Memorial Day through Labor Day.

What to Expect

•Entry to the interpretive trail of the park requires a U.S. Forest Service pass, which you can buy for three dollars from the park host.

Things to Know

•The dysentery that plagued Elizabeth's wagon train inflames the intestine, causing high fever, abdominal cramps, and painful diarrhea. Infants, the elderly, and the malnourished are especially vulnerable.

•According to one source, Forest Service archeologists have identified at least five pioneer graves in the park.

Who to Contact

•For more information, call the Wallowa-Whitman National Forest at 541-963-7186.

Elgin-Weston

Across the Blue Mountains of northeast Oregon lies a centuries-old trail that has seen the passing of pack trains and the coming of diesel trucks. Indian tribes, fur trappers, cavalry patrols, freight wagons, stagecoaches—all used the route to travel between the Grande Ronde and Walla Walla valleys.

At least, they used it during the warm months, for this is a fair-weather road. Even today in these mountains of gusting wind and lingering shade, of sno-parks and dog-hair thickets, the snowplows and blowdowns of winter change the pass into a high-walled luge run. Summer, however, changes all that.

"Once the snow melts, it's a mountain range you can ride a bicycle over," says a man who's done it. Sounds like a nutty idea.

Of course, you can drive the mountain road that connects the towns of Elgin and Weston, but if the urge strikes you to leave your car behind, a good reason to begin at Elgin is that you'll climb almost 1,000 feet less than if you begin at the other end. Enough said.

Elgin is a town with a population of about 1,500 located on the banks of the Grande Ronde River. A favorite gathering and fishing place of the Nez Perce, this area was once called either Indian Valley or Fishtrap. Later it became an important freight hub for the Walla Walla, Grande Ronde, and Wallowa Valleys. Near the middle of its downtown is the junction of Highway 204, which is your passageway over the Blues.

At the other end, 41 miles away, is Weston, but the summit is less than half that distance away. In addition, you'll find this bit of justice in the journey. It gets cooler as you climb, the temperature 10 to 20 degrees lower on top than it is at the bottom.

Until you get close to the summit, that bottom has the flattest grade you'll find as the road cuts its way through the stream bed of Phillips Creek, which flows through the wedge of a v-shaped canyon where the morning sun touches only the tips of the trees. Long curves sweep past pines and firs and cottonwoods on its shady way into the Umatilla National Forest, where mock orange and elderberry line the stream.

Although some of the mileposts are missing, probably knocked over by snowplows, the ones left can help you plot your course. (The zero point is the highway junction near Weston.) For instance, you can plan breaks at the larger turnouts and sno-parks near mileposts 32 and 29, or find a glimmer of hope at milepost 28—Summit Road. The road doesn't really mark the summit, but it's close, and a few flats and downhills from here give you a break from the climb. You'll find another kind of break near milepost 26—a restroom at Andies Prairie.

From Andies Prairie is a three mile stretch to the summit, taking you past a viewpoint overlooking the headwaters of the Umatilla River, then the turnoff to Woodland Campground, and finally the top of the grade—5,158 feet. Darn near a mile high.

The downhill run takes you past Spout Springs, one of the oldest ski resorts in the Northwest—now closed—and then through a stretch of rolling hills and across the Umatilla County line, where the forest thins and the sunlight spots the pavement. The halfway point of the trip is Tollgate, now a resort area but once a critical stop on the old wagon road.

Yes, there really was a toll gate at Tollgate. A private company built the twenty-mile road in 1873-74 for a cost of about $2,500. Evidently, it was a bargain. An 1872 edition of the *Walla Walla Union* newspaper said this road "would add more to the business prosperity of this city than any other work that could be accomplished with the same amount of money."

But because of the long winters, the road was usually open for only five months a year, from June through October. Even then,

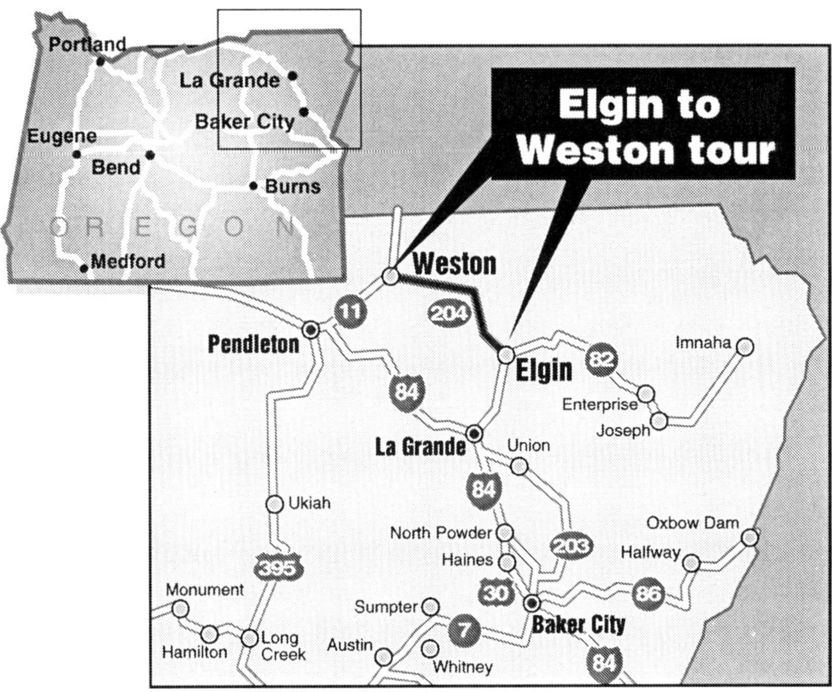

freight and stage drivers sometimes had to wrap their horses' feet in gunny sacks to keep them from sinking through the snow.

Nearby is Langdon Lake, formed long ago when John Langdon dammed Looking Glass Creek.The water now covers the site of the farm and hotel once operated by the toll road manager.

Down the road is a small place with a big name—The Tollgate Shopping Center and Restaurant. If you want something to eat, this is your best chance on the mountain. (A few miles ahead is the Tollgate Mountain Chalet, but don't count on it being open.) From here begins a sharp downhill run to a viewpoint, and then on past weekend cabins set in a ragged forest on the edge of canyon lands.

In these foothills of the Blues, the air carries the sharp, dry scent of herbs just before you leave the shade, hit the grassland, and see the haze of the Walla Walla Valley in the distance. Because you'll get direct sunlight here, the temperature will continue to rise as you drop toward the valley floor.

When the landscape shifts from pine green to wheat brown, you'll probably find the sun glaring, the air warming, the road winding downhill sharp and fast—and you'll see why you didn't start your ride from the other direction.

Between mileposts 3 and 2 look for Kirk Road. This is the old road into Weston. Follow it down through its hills and draws and locust groves; watch for whitetail deer in the fields, valley quail near the blackberries. Then when you drop into Weston, population 620, head for the Long Branch, pardner.

This restaurant and watering hole, built in 1874 from bricks made in the local brickyards, has watched more than a century of Weston history pass by its doors. Once a thriving trade center for Umatilla County's farming communities, Weston at the turn of the century was a town of six churches, six mercantiles, four saloons, two hotels, and a train depot. In those days, tree-lined Main Street framed a cherub-topped central fountain fed by a mountain spring.

Today the highway has moved and the fountain is gone, but the Long Branch remains. This is a place where the waitress might call you Hon—as in "What'll it be, Hon?"—and the sandwiches have

Where to Go

•From Interstate 84, take Exit 261 at La Grande, then follow Highway 82 for 19 miles to Elgin.

When to Go

•On weekdays, the highway usually carries more trucks than cars; on weekends, more cars than trucks.

Things to Know

•Elgin was named for a song, "Lost on the Lady Elgin," which the first postmaster heard his niece and nephew singing. The song tells the story of the 1860 wreck of the steamship Lady Elgin on Lake Michigan.

•Weston was named for its first postmaster's hometown, Weston, Missouri.

•The climb from Weston (elevation 1,838 feet) to the summit is 3,320 feet; from Elgin (2,716 feet) to the summit, 2442 feet.

Who to Contact

•To make sure you find a seat at the Long Branch, you might want to call for a reservation at 541-566-3478.

names such as "Miss Kitty" and "Marshall Dillon." Even the "Kitty" and "Festus" labels on the restroom doors are in character.

This is also a place where the people at the next table might strike up a conversation. "I'll tell you," says a man sitting at one of those tables, "this is the right place to come if you're hungry." And it's good to know that after riding over a mountain range, you've come to the right place.

Flagstaff Hill

At the now famous National Historic Oregon Trail Interpretive Center outside Baker City, most people catch only a glimpse through glass of a pioneer purgatory. That's because most visitors confine themselves to the view from the picture windows of the center's main building. Yet the dust-breathing, sore-footed trudge of the emigrants happened on the other side of the plate glass, on the sagebrush slopes that roll their way down to the Powder River in the distance.

For those who want to experience this part of the emigrants' world, the Flagstaff Hill Loop Trail weaves through a good chunk of the 500 acres making up the center's grounds. The different historic sites and viewpoints along this trail show you one of the paths the pioneers followed and some of the country they saw.

"The hike gives you a way to get a feel for the country," says a man along the trail. "And it's something you just can't find inside the Interpretive Center itself." (Other things you won't find inside are the heat, ticks, mosquitoes, rattlesnakes, and scorpions you might meet if you wander off the trail, especially in spring and summer. Obviously, this hike requires some pioneer spirit.)

Consisting of a number of loops of varying lengths, the four mile trail system leads you on a tour of the emigrants' route after

they made the arduous ascent of the Burnt River and pushed ahead toward the Powder River Valley. Even though houses and ranches and roads now sprawl across this valley, enough of the wild is left to show you what it was like in the days of the wagon trains.

"The trail system beckons to visitors who want to step into history and walk the way of the pioneers," says the Bureau of Land Management, which manages the site.

The top level of the system is a half-mile circle around the hilltop Interpretive Center. Along this paved path is a replica of an emigrant camp, complete with wagons and campfires. You'll also find views southeast to Virtue Flat, a desert the emigrants were glad to escape, and west to the Blue Mountains, a barrier they would have to cross before winter. But in-between was the valley the emigrants called Lone Pine, for the single tree that once grew there.

"The Tree is a large Pine standing in the midst of an immense plain entirely alone," wrote an 1842 emigrant. "It presented a truly singular appearance and I believe is respected by every traveler through this almost Treeless Country."

From the top of the hill, two trails lead down the slope—the Ascent Trail (unpaved) and the Panorama Trail (paved). Because of their different surfaces and levels of difficulty, the BLM recommends—now get your thinking caps out for this—that you first descend on the Ascent Trail. Go figure. In addition, the numbers on the trail's interpretive signs, which match the guide book, follow in sequence only if you descend on the Panorama Trail.

So if you follow that sequence and take the asphalt down to the next level of the trail system, you'll find Panorama Point, which gives perhaps the best view of the area. A three-quarter mile hike takes you not only to the Point, but also past the same kinds of sagebrush and bunchgrass that grew in this area more than a century ago, before the days of widespread grazing and Smoky the Bear.

Along the treeless length of the trail, the only protection from the weather are a few post-and-beam shelters. Although the shade these provide is important during the summer when temperatures can hit 100 degrees, during the fall and winter they make good sit-down-and-stare-at-the-view seats. This is especially true at the Point

Where to Go

•From Interstate 84, take Exit 302 and follow the signs east on Highway 86.

When to Go

•The trail system closes at 6 p.m. from April 1 to October 31, and at 4 p.m. from November 1 to March 31.

What to Expect

•Admission to the center is five dollars per person or ten dollars per car.

•Trail guides are available in the Interpretive Center.

Things to Know

•After arriving in the Northwest, Ezra Meeker became the nation's most successful hop grower. You can still find his house in Puyallup, Washington, the city he founded.

Who to Contact

•For more information, call the BLM's Baker City office at 541-523-1843.

itself, where you'll find a large gazeboesque building overlooking the Oregon Trail. From here you can gaze out over the slopes the wagons traveled and the valley the emigrants sought.

The remains from other periods of history are also visible from here. One is the 1862 wagon road to the Auburn gold mines. This trail junction was an important crossroads, a place of separation for many of the wagons because while some continued on to the Willamette or Walla Walla valleys, others turned off to the mines.

"I must confess we felt lonesome and bad as we bid adieu to friends that had crossed the extended plains with us that stood by us in the hour of danger & had traveled together for 5 month," wrote an 1862 emigrant. "They seemed near to us in deed & many a tear was shed at our separation."

The outdoor centerpiece of this Oregon Trail complex, however, is farther down the path, almost 400 feet lower than the Interpretive Center and less than a half mile away from Panorama Point—the wagon ruts themselves. Thousands of iron-rimmed wheels cut the slope here, creating billowing dust at the time and an enduring memorial thereafter.

Another kind of memorial stands nearby, Ezra Meeker's granite marker. Meeker, who made the trip west by wagon in 1852, decided in 1906 to walk the Trail backwards, setting out markers as he made his way east. He was 76 years old at the time. Appropriately, this is the place where the pavement ends, for here the Ascent Trail begins its steep climb back to the Interpretive Center along an unpaved, rock-strewn, water-rutted path.

When you reach the top of the slope and find a bank of spotting scopes—which means you could have gazed down at the ruts from the comfort of the parking lot, could have saved your shoes and your sweat—you can be glad you took the walk, for you saw from ground level a part of the pioneers' world that few ever experience.

Hat Rock

Unframe the houses and unwhistle the trains—let your imagination do this upstream of McNary Dam, and you're left with a trail that pulls you back to an unmapped Oregon and a wild Columbia river. This pathway is the Lake Wallula Scenic River Trail, a secluded area set aside for hiking, biking, hunting, fishing, and birding.

A good place to get on the trail is at Hat Rock State Park, located nine miles east of Umatilla on Highway 730. The park's namesake is the remnant of a basalt flow left exposed when the Lake Missoula floods carved out the Columbia Gorge and flooded the plateau during the last ice age. Some time later, the rock caught the attention of Meriwether Lewis.

Near this spot almost 200 years ago, the Pacific-bound Corps of Discovery found four islands, twelve houses, and "a bad rapid...At the foot of this rapid is a rock, on the left shore, which...resembles a hat in its shape."

Although the rapids and islands lie now under the slack water of Wallula Lake, which covers 62 miles of the Columbia's 1,214 mile course, the rock remains. Many compare the formation to a man's top hat, but others disagree.

"Looks more like a derby to me," says a woman on one of the paths that leads through the sage and up toward the rock. When she points toward it, she seems to be waving to the backyards of the houses squeezing the park boundary. "The basalt is its crown and the hill is the brim."

But no matter what kind of hat it resembles, the rock overlooks almost 800 acres of river-edged park, where every day of the year you can picnic and fish, boat and hike. Its centerpiece is a spring-fed pond near the boat launching area.

Surrounded by a footpath and crossed with an arched bridge, the pond is noisy with the splash, quacks and chirps of geese, mallards and widgeons. Along its curved shore are shaded picnic tables. And on the flat rim above the nearby parking lot is the trail.

From here, the Lake Wallula Scenic River Trail (some maps label it the Hat Rock Scenic Corridor) skirts past the park and winds through a primitive land of sage and sand, rock and water. Along the bank of the Northwest's largest river is one of its driest climates, and the trail is part of the Corps of Engineers' effort to give the region "an abundance of public recreational opportunities" after damming this stretch of river into a lake that would help water the desert. (Running beneath this lake from Umatilla to Pasco is a river channel five feet deep and 100 feet wide.)

"I think it's an old railroad grade," says a man strolling with his wife near the trail's entrance. Binoculars hang from his neck. He mentions that since their retirement, they spend a lot of time wandering the trail.

"Don't know how far it goes," the woman says. "We've gone a long ways up but never reached the end." The end is almost five miles away, downstream at McNary Beach.

Between park and beach lies a gravel path that curves around slopes and rolls over hills while it leads you along the river. Although the Corps of Engineers manages the trail for multiple use, it draws the line at motor vehicles; if you go, it's by bike, foot, or horse power only.

"Once on the trail, you've made a commitment," says Pasquale Anolfo, whose job includes patrolling the area for the McNary Project. "The only way to get off is to reach the end or turn around."

And because the trail cuts through thirsty, secluded country-side in which summer temperatures can top 100 degrees, you have to pack what you need. Along the way you'll find no drinking water, restrooms or shade, but you will encounter deer tracks and

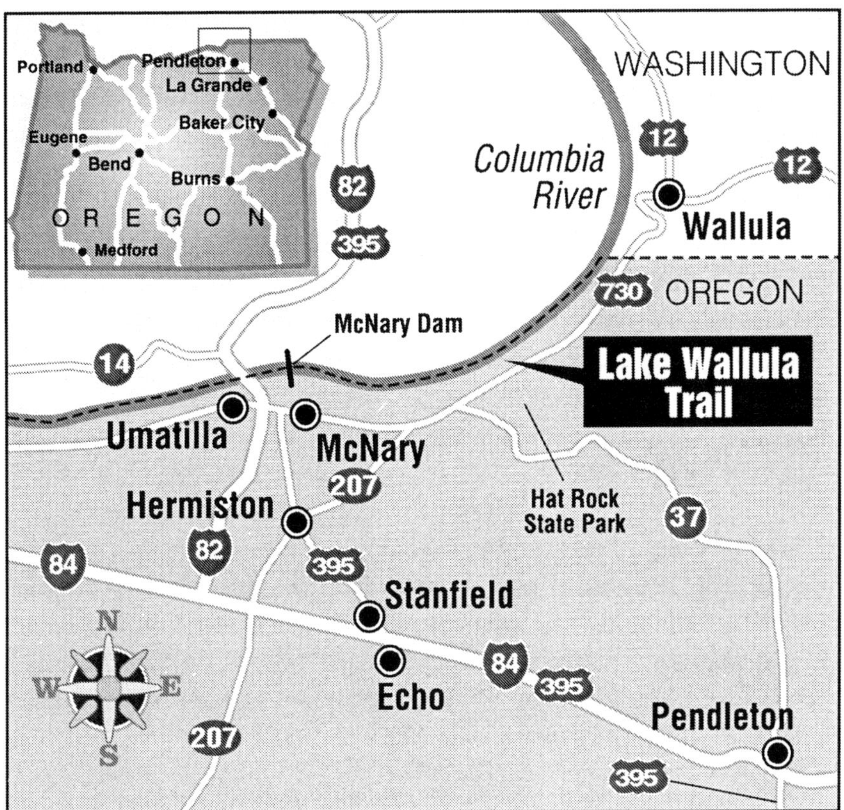

Where to Go

•From Interstate 84, take Exit 182 or 188 to Hermiston. To enter the trail at McNary Beach, drive north on Highway 395; to enter at Hat Rock State Park, drive northeast on Highway 207.

Things to Know

•After sighting Hat Rock on October 19, 1805, Lewis and Clark reached the ocean 19 days later, on November 7.

•McNary Dam's reservoir is 340 feet above sea level, but irrigating much of the plateau above the river requires pumping to at least 1,000 feet. This uses approximately one third of the power generated by the dam.

Who to Contact

•For more information about the park, call 541-567-5032.

•For more information about the trail, call 541-922-4388.

coyote droppings, ant hills and meadowlarks—and a good chance of having the place to yourself.

"The trail doesn't get a lot of use," Anolfo says. "But it's a nice place to take a walk, go hunting or fishing."

It's also a great place for sightseeing. Although the Corps of Engineers has changed the river since the Corps of Discovery first saw it, the mountains of the Cascade Range haven't moved.

In the same journal entry that describes Hat Rock, Meriwether Lewis mentions Mount St. Helens ("To the west at the distance of about one hundred and fifty miles, is a very high mountain covered with snow...") as well as Mount Hood ("...there is also another mountain of a conical form, whose top is covered with snow, in a southwest direction.")

In the other direction, however, is a different kind of looming presence. Perched on the rim above the trail are the roofs of a housing development. But this you leave behind when you pass through a gate and hike into the Columbia Basin Wildlife Area. From here only an occasional train whistle on the Washington side of the river pulls you away from thoughts of a Lewis and Clark flotilla rounding the bend.

If you wander toward the water, you'll hike through sage and wildflowers while listening to the breeze-blown Columbia wash against its bank. Before summer heat makes the slopes shimmer, this is a gentle place where moss, soft as pillows, grows on the river-side of lichen-flaked rocks.

Near one of those rocks, the man with the binoculars stops to glass a yellow-bellied marmot. "Someday," his wife says, "we're going to pack a lunch and some folding chairs and walk to the end of this trail."

To show the man was right about the railroad, in the trail nearby lies a rail spike, rusted and pitted with age, but still a newcomer to an area where Lewis and Clark found homes and rapids—and a hat-shaped rock that would someday become the gateway to a wilder past.

Imnaha Canyon

As Captain Benjamin Bonneville discovered in 1834—when he floundered through this area, lost and reduced to eating his mules before the Nez Perce rescued him—when you set out to explore the Snake River country in the far northeast corner of Oregon, you'd better know where the heck you're going.

The land that almost swallowed the good captain is today part of the Hells Canyon National Recreation Area (HCNRA), more than 650,000 acres created by Congress in 1975 to preserve what was left of the undammed, free flowing portion of the Snake River. Shared by Oregon and Idaho, the remote land is a panorama of canyon walls, mountain slopes, and bench lands that edge the Imnaha and Snake Rivers.

But while the Snake draws attention for its world-class whitewater and its mile-deep gorge, the Imnaha is a homegrown stream, winding its way through Wallowa County's Eagle Cap Wilderness before reaching civilization at Imnaha—a one-school, one-church community found at the end of a 30 mile stretch of State Scenic Byway that drops two thousand feet from its beginning at Joseph. Located on the banks of the Imnaha River, the town is the starting point for those explorers who are willing to leave the pavement behind as they hike, bike, or drive through the canyon.

"The area contains some of the most breathtaking country in the West," says Frank Conley, who operates tours along the Imnaha River. He also adds that a reasonable range of adventure can take you from four feet to four miles.

For example, a four-foot hike will almost get you through the door of the Imnaha Store and Tavern, once the home of the Annual Bear and Rattlesnake Feed, the community's top social event of the year. Even though that celebration is now defunct, you can still order a platter of chicken gizzards and a glass of cold beer. On the other hand, a four mile hike—following a fifteen mile drive, most of it on either dirt or gravel—will get you down the Cow Creek trail all the way to the Snake River.

And between the gizzards and the Snake is a land that is steppe and desert, rim and river; an area that is home at one time or another during the year to more than 350 species of wildlife. The main reason for the variety and number of canyon critters is what the U.S. Forest Service calls, "one of the most varied habitats in the nation."

In the canyon you'll find the hills layered and stacked to the horizon; the slopes covered with crumbled rock and red soil, spotted with grass or sage or sumac; the draws trickling water and growing thick with cottonwoods and hackberry. Here wildflowers sprout next to sagebrush, and the prickly pear of the desert grows near the Douglas fir of the coast. And through it all runs the river. The wildlife seems to love it.

On a recent tour along the Imnaha River Road, Conley's group encountered golden eagles, red-tailed hawks, ospreys, deer, otters, raccoons, and bighorn sheep. "The sheep were right down along the road," he says. "We could have almost reached out the car window and petted them."

What you see depends on where you go from Imnaha—upriver toward the timber and several trailheads; downriver toward the Snake and the entrance to the HCNRA; or uphill to Hat Point, the easternmost point in Oregon and, at almost seven thousand feet, the highest viewpoint around.

If you had to choose a season to visit the canyon, it would probably be either when the wildflowers are growing in spring or the leaves are turning in fall. "Fall is definitely the season for the best weather and the most spectacular scenery," Conley says.

By then the summer heat, which makes the canyon walls glare and shimmer, is tipping away, cooling down; the mosquitoes and

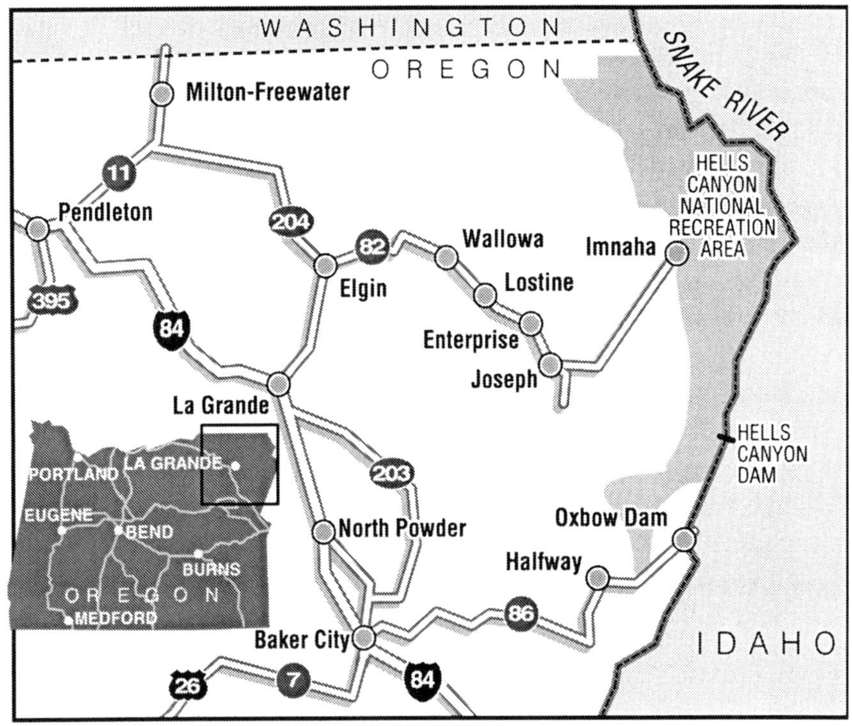

Where to Go

•From Interstate 84, take Exit 261 at La Grande, then follow Highway 82 for 70 miles to Joseph. Imnaha is 30 miles east of town.

What to Expect

•Learn to say Imnaha: im-NAW-haw.

•If it rains, don't attempt to drive the Imnaha River Road. (The names for the road's gumbo mud is unprintable.) Instead, wait it out in town and get yourself some of those gizzards.

Who to Contact

•For more information, call HCNRA headquarters at 541-426-4978.

rattlers and poison oak have tucked themselves in. Meanwhile, the autumn light makes the sky shine blue and turns the hillsides red and yellow.

In addition, the Imnaha autumn seems to linger, squeezing winter out until the last possible moment. The Nez Perce, who used the canyon as their winter home for ten thousand years, used this fact to their advantage. So did the late nineteenth and early twentieth century homesteaders, sheepmen, cowboys, and miners who once tried to scratch out a living here.

In the early part of this century, a Hells Canyon settler described her neighbors' feelings for the land. "They were conscious of the beauty about them, the songs of birds, the melody of the mountain streams," she wrote. "And as they filled their lungs with the sweet, fresh pine scented air, their hearts responded, 'This is the life!'"

This is a feeling still shared by many who enter the canyon of the Imnaha River. As Conley says to people who are about to see it for the first time: "Your view of the world will never be quite the same!"

As for Captain Bonneville, he survived the effects of his mule meat diet, though the reports of the hardships he suffered in the Snake River country discouraged travelers from entering the area for quite some time. Consequently, for many years the canyons of the Snake and its tributaries remained unexplored, almost unknown. Even at the turn of the century, a homesteader found this place to be "a lonely, untamed region." Luckily for today's explorers, it still is.

Ladd Marsh Wildlife Area

At the turn of the century, folks in this country were crazy about birds, especially on hats. Birds skinned, stuffed, and plucked decorated the tops of women's heads, and the killing of birds for their feathers, plumes, or meat became big business. Some people, however, believed that watching birds was preferable to shooting them. And when the bird watchers stopped the market hunters, artificial flowers replaced bird feathers (on hats, not on birds).

The result today is a national bird population of six billion—which figures out to about three birds per acre or 23 birds per person. In Oregon, one of the best places to see your share is the Ladd Marsh Wildlife Area, located five miles south of La Grande in northeastern Oregon.

With more than 3,000 acres of grass and water, this chunk of the Grande Ronde Valley is one of the largest remaining wetlands in the region and serves as an occasional home for almost 170 species of birds. "Ladd Marsh is the center of birding in the Grande Ronde Valley," says Gina Hart, one of the valley's most enthusiastic birders. "In the winter you'll find ducks, geese, and other migratory birds; in the spring and summer, you'll find more passerines—perching birds."

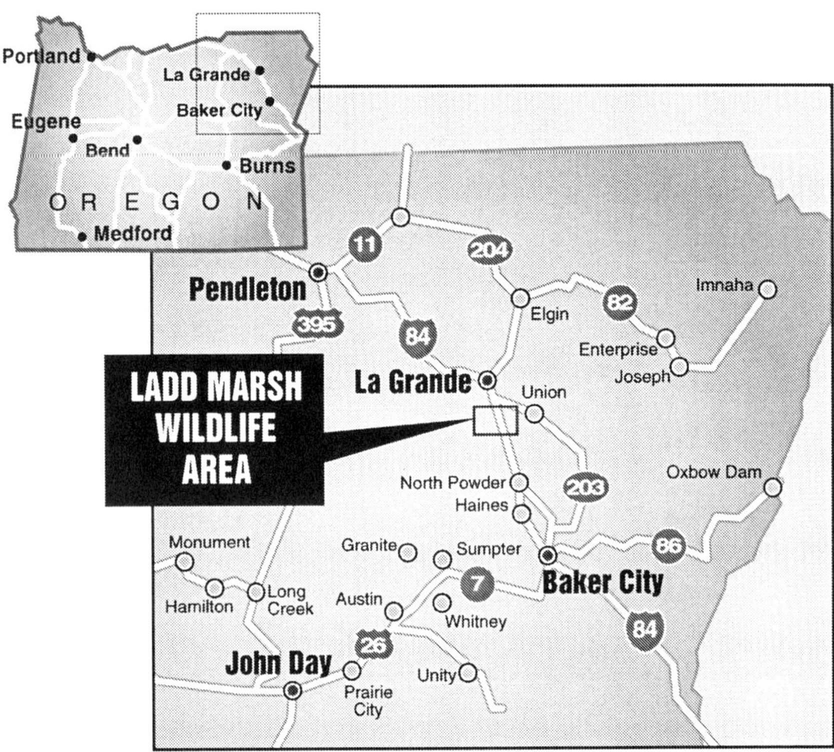

Forming part of the marsh's western boundary is Foothill Road, which offers the best viewing area. From here you can look out across a land of fields and fence rows, ponds and marshes, rail fences and wind breaks. If you're willing to walk, you'll find another viewpoint south of here, at Oxen Springs, an unmarked section of the wildlife area on the hill above the road.

According to some local historians, a spring in this area is where pioneers stopped to reshod their oxen after coming down the steep and rocky slope of nearby Ladd Canyon. Now this old resting place is gnarled with thickets of old apple and plum orchards and brambles of wild roses.

A trail cuts through here, though, and as you follow an old stone wall, you'll step over deer tracks and coyote droppings, cross seasonal springs, watch squirrels peek out of kestrel boxes. On the edge of the valley are the mountains Harris and Emily; in the distance, the snow-capped Wallowas. And usually there is wind. Pioneer diaries rarely mention it, but the Grande Ronde is a valley of wind that can make trees roar.

Across the interstate is the road to Hot Lake. Near the ruins of the old hotel, steam rises and drifts from the eight-acre lake fed by the largest hot spring of its kind in the world. In the early 1800s, fur trappers passing through this area found hundreds of elk antlers lying near the mineral pool, leading them to believe that this was a wintering area for elk. Now it's a winter home for ducks.

"This is the best duck loop," Hart says, adding that even more ducks visit in the spring than in the winter. This is because Ladd Marsh sprawls along the edge of an ice-age lake, and during each spring thaw, the valley seems to remember this. "In the spring, a lot of this area is flooded," Hart says, "and the ducks come in by the thousands." But there's good reason to visit the marsh in the fall and winter, for it's the only time you can enter it without a special permit.

Because the refuge is supported largely by the money generated through hunting licenses, the only times it's open to the public is Wednesdays, weekends, and holidays through the

Where to Go

•From Interstate 84 near La Grande, take Exit 265 or 268.

What to Expect

•Because the area is without hiking paths—except for the Nature Trail on its border—you'll want to wear boots that take the slosh out of walking.

•If you go in the spring, summer, or fall, take along a mountain bike. Roads surrounding the wildlife area are easily accessible and have little traffic.

Things to Know

•Birdwatching has replaced fishing as America's primary recreation.

•Oregon is home to about 360 of the 9,000 species of birds in the world.

•Every 24 hours, two and one half million gallons of 186 degree water bubbles out of the ground at Hot Lake.

Who to Contact

•For more information, call the Wildlife Area at 541-963-4954.

pheasant and waterfowl seasons.The rest of the time, it's reserved for the birds. So unless you want to stay on the road and cruise the perimeter, you'll want to plan your visit for hunting season, even if you don't want to shoot anything but photographs. Another good reason for a winter visit is the Christmas Bird Count.

To understand this count, it's necessary to go back to the bad old days of plumed hats, when market hunters slaughtered birds for money.Yet other people had different reasons for killing birds. For example, the *side hunt* was a popular holiday event of the nineteenth century. This was a Christmas time competition that pitted teams against each other in the field, with the team killing the most birds winning the contest.

This killing so disturbed a fellow named Frank Chapman that on Christmas day of 1900, he staged a protest against it by gathering some friends, going into the field—and counting all the birds they could find.

Then it was a novel idea; now it's a traditional event held throughout the entire Western Hemisphere and involving more than 45,000 volunteers in approximately 1700 counts. "The Christmas Bird Count has evolved into the largest and longest running wildlife survey ever undertaken," says the National Audubon Society, the event's sponsor

Why count birds in the first place? One reason is the canary-in-the-mine idea. "Birds are indicators of the overall health of our environment," says the Audubon. This means that the Christmas Count can give us information about how both the birds and our world are doing. But another reason is less dramatic. It's fun. As an excuse to get outside or a cure for cabin fever, winter birding is tough to beat. And the Christmas Bird Count adds an element of sociability."With a group," Hart says,"you have a shared enthusiasm."

Even though we no longer wear birds on our hats, millions of people are still crazy about them—birds that sing, swim, soar and strut; perching birds and game birds, shore birds and raptors. And finding birds in winter seems especially important, some birders say, because it's as though the world is keeping its promise that spring will come again.

Sheep Rock Trails

Someone stole the stabbing cat. Someone unbolted the steel frame, broke the Plexiglas cover, and pulled the cat from its 25 million year old bed. But if the grave robbers had taken the time to read the sign, they would have known the fossilized cat, which once terrorized resident herbivores, was a replica. The real fossil is down the road at the John Day Fossil Beds visitors center in eastern Oregon.

Animals such as the stabbing cat have been lying about the fossil beds for as long as 60 million years, yet it took early paleontologists until the 1860s to find the place. That's when Thomas Condon, an early Oregon settler and Congregational minister, recognized the importance of what lies buried along the John Day River, a priceless record of life on earth.

Although it took more than a century after Condon's work for the federal government to designate the area a National Monument, today the 14,000 acres making up its three units provide visitors with a chance to see one of the most important fossil beds in the world.

To do this, you don't have to know the difference between Oligocene and Pliocene or between brontotheres and amynonts; you don't have to speak Latin or understand rocks. You need only a sense of wonder and adventure, and a way to get to the Sheep Rock Unit, which is a good starting point for a variety of trails that will take you on a hike through time.

Blue Basin Area

This area consists of two trails—one long, one short. The long one is the Blue Basin Overlook Trail, which involves a three mile hike up and around a canyon. It's wise to heed the advice on the "Trailhead Orientation" sign and tackle the trail in a clockwise direction, for this sends you downhill on the steepest of the 600 foot slopes. Also good advice is the warning about packing water, wearing a hat, and watching for snakes.

At the outset, you'll walk a gravel path that bends through head-high sagebrush as it takes you along the edge of green-faced hills, across a green-stained stream, and into the rock and grass and juniper of the canyon wall.

Soon the trail climbs higher, the stream cuts deeper, the canyon grows narrower; the junipers thicken and the sagebrush recedes as you tread on red-veined rock past Russian olives and cottonwoods, bunchgrass and yarrow. In places where the canyon tries to sluff the trail from its slope, rocks and boards shore up the path and hold back the mud.

Near the head of the canyon, a series of switchbacks steers you toward a bench sitting on a stone base and overlooking the canyon. "Time is lost and years are but the pulse beat," is part of the message on a nearby sign. This is appropriate about now, an hour into the hike, for your own pulse beat may well be thudding in your ears. Between beats, however, listen for ravens and chukars calling in the distance.

"This is really worth the climb," says a man sitting on the bench and fiddling with his camera. He gazes toward the John Day River below. "It's so beautiful here."

A striking part of that beauty is up on the rim, where a viewpoint above Blue Basin shows you a landscape of chasms and columns, of spires and slopes; a country of rock and sky and red rolling hills. It's a place difficult to leave.

But when you do, you'll find the trail curving downhill, crossing for a stretch through private property, then cutting its way through what's left of the spring's wildflowers—phlox, delphinium, Indian paint brush. This route gives you a wide-open view of the river valley as it sends you down the steep, short turns of a switchback, back to the bottom and the beginning of the short trail—the Island in Time Trail.

This route takes you a half mile into Blue Basin, giving you a close-up view of what the longer trail showed you from a distance. "There are ghosts in Blue Basin," the sign tells you. And the trail takes you to them.

The packed gravel path follows a lime-green trickle of a stream, crosses footbridges, and courses past shelves of rock holding slopes of scree and layers of time—30 million years of time. That's when nearby volcanic eruptions began burying this land in ash, building the blue-green beds that now form the canyon walls.

Those volcanoes also settled an ash blanket over the remains of the plants and animals that once lived in that long-ago land, and instead of decaying, they fossilized, their bones or their wood filling with minerals. Then wind and water not only carved the basin, but also unearthed its fossils.

You can still see the claw marks of time along the gouged walls that seem to be dripping rock, and as you walk toward the amphitheater at trail's end, you'll see the encased remains of a tortoise and an oreodont—a sheep-sized, leaf-eating mammal that was the favorite prey of the sabertooth cat. Of course, the stabbing cat is gone.

Foree Area

This area consists of two quarter-mile trails—the Story in Stone Trail and the Flood of Fire Trail. Great names, interesting trails—but no highway sign to mark them. So instead, look for a paved side road about five miles from the Blue Basin trailhead, take a right, and drive a half mile. This should put you in a paved parking lot with picnic tables, restrooms, and interpretive signs.

At one of those signs is a booklet that gives you a self-guided tour of the Story in Stone Trail, a half-paved, half-gravel pathway that gives you basic lessons in the rocks and fossils and animals of the area, going back some 30 million years.

On the other side of the parking lot, the Flood of Fire Trail takes you up a slight slope to a view of what's left from a 16 million year old event. And the sign explaining this phenomenon should receive a reward for literary merit. Here's part of it:

"With no explosive warning, no sign of volcanic cones or smoke, the lava gushed from narrow fissures and poured almost as fast as water across this land, forming huge lakes of molten rock...All life in the area must have been suddenly wiped out by the relentless flows." Darn good writing for a government agency, don't you think?

Anyway, that's the way it happened millions of years ago in this place of bones, where time passes like a shadow, and trails lead to a sense of eternity. And in this way, there is no trail's end.

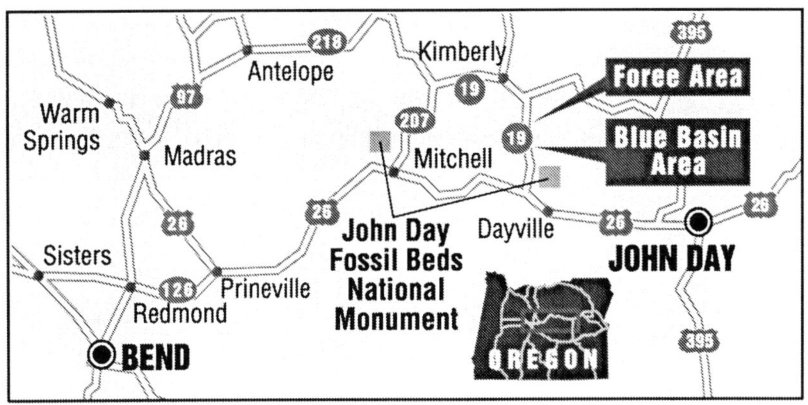

Where to Go

•The entrance to the Sheep Rock Unit is at the intersection of U.S. Highway 26 and Oregon Highway 19, six miles west of Dayville. The Blue Basin Area is five miles north.

When to Go

•From March through October the visitor center is open daily; the rest of the year it's open Monday through Friday, except on holidays. Trails and picnic areas are open year round.

Things to Know

•Thomas Condon, Oregon's first state geologist, named the fossil beds "Turtle Cove."

•John Day was a Virginian who came to Oregon with the 1811-12 Astor-Hunt expedition. The river may be named for him because near its mouth he and another man were attacked and robbed by Indians, then stripped naked and left in the wild.

Who to Contact

•For more information, call the visitors center at 541-987-2333.

Snake River Road

As its waters flow from the Rockies to the Columbia, the Snake River changes both its face and its job many times. From alpine stream to desert canal, from canyon carver to flaccid reservoir, the Snake slides and curls its way through the West, entering Oregon as a watering trough for high desert farms, and leaving it as a roiling runaway from Hells Canyon dams.

The roughest stretch of water, some of the old rivermen claimed, flowed between Farewell Bend, Oregon, and Lewiston, Idaho; now the dams make a long section of that run one of the tamest. Even so, a journey along the Snake River Road offers one of the longest and closest views of the river you can get by car.

"The drive along the Snake from Richland to Huntington offers some beautiful geology and geography," says a woman who knows the country. "It's fun, too, to imagine living out there in the old, pre-highway days."

Fun to imagine but tough to do, for this is raw, rugged country built from steep rock and deep water. The best view along the road's 42 miles begins just outside the town of Richland in northeast Oregon's Baker County. From here the road heads south through Eagle Valley and up toward the flat-topped hills bordering Eagle Creek and leading to the Snake.

Three miles from Richland the pavement ends, and from near the summit of the gravel road you can look down into the creased bottoms of hills rolling brown and gold with grass and sage and wildflowers. In the distance are the green sparkle of Eagle Valley and the white caps of the Wallowa Mountains.

Just up the road is the Richland Overlook, which gives you a striking view of the river, its banks etched with high water marks like the rings around a bathtub. But even if the water here is calmed into a gray-green reservoir by Brownlee Dam, the canyon is still untamed—deep cut and far reaching, its walls folded into draws and buckled beneath ridges.

Down and across one of those slopes cuts the road, and you'd better have good brakes for the drop to the river's edge, which you reach ten miles from the end of the pavement. Once off the rim, you may find the drama of the canyon diminished, for the river seems to crawl instead of flow, though it still pushes enough current to gouge the banks and scar its flanks.

The next five miles upstream takes you through a monochromatic land of brown, the air carrying the scents of dusty alkali and still water, the scenery seeming to sag along—the power lines over the road, the road along the river, the river through its canyon. Then when the river bed widens, its water forms into a long lake with a serpentine shoreline holding campgrounds, cabins, and boat launches.

In spite of the development, you'll once again find the wild mixing with the tame. Sipping from hillside springs are sumac and locusts, Russian olives and cottonwoods; swooping along the slopes are chukars, doves, and kestrels. Still, from this point on lies a section of the road that people can't seem to agree on.

"It's not nearly as wild down here," says a woman driving the road. "The people who camp here must like it open, barren, and hot—though the ground would be soft beneath a sleeping bag."

"Looks like the place where old trailers go to die," says a man stopped along the road and gazing over the trailer-cluttered slope leading to the river.

But others have a positive—and practical—view of this part of the Snake. "I always envied those rugged, adventuresome homesteading women," says a woman who lives in Richland. "But no doubt it had some downsides along with the mystic. For instance, some of those cranky old husbands must have been like broncos

with a burr under their saddle when they ran short of booze."

No matter how people react to it, the Bureau of Land Management thinks this road is important enough to list it as part of its National Back Country Byways program. One of its attractions, says the BLM, is that you can "wet your line in one of the best warm water fisheries in the west." Those fish include bluegill, crappie, and perch. But along this part of the Snake, it means catfish.

Because they enjoy a typical year-round season with no catch limits, many catfishers visit the slackwater Snake during all four seasons. You can recognize them by their traditional equipment—for sitting, lawn chairs and rod holders; for fishing, spark plugs for weight and chicken livers or night crawlers for bait. Although it's enough to make some flyfishing purists wince, catfishing has it share of staunch devotees.

"There's nothing better than fresh catfish cooked outdoors over an open fire," says a woman who fishes the Snake. "But you can't be in a hurry. You plunk your bait out there and wait, and you never know what's going to be on the end of the line when you reel it in. That's what makes it fun."

Some think it's so much fun that the downstream town of Huntington—the end of the Snake River Road—bills itself as "The Catfishing Capital of Oregon." In addition, a few years ago a petition circulating in Huntington businesses argued that the river's catfish would be threatened if the government went ahead with plans to restore the Snake's salmon.

Maybe the river can never be again what it was in the time of the salmon, in the days before the dams rose and the river slowed. But a leisurely drive along its banks can still show you signs of the Snake now sleeping beneath its own still waters.

Where to Go

- You can travel the Snake River Road starting at either Huntington (take Exit 345 on Interstate 84) or Richland (take Exit 302, then drive 38 miles east on Highway 86).
- You'll find a few campgrounds along the road, at least one with a restroom.

What to Expect

- In spring, wildflowers; in summer, heat; in fall and winter, chukars.

Things to Know

- The Bureau of Land Management's Back Country Byways in Oregon includes 13 routes covering over 750 miles.
- Although the Snake River/Mormon Basin Back Country Byway includes the Richland to Huntington road, the entire byway covers a 130 mile loop.

Who to Contact

- For more information about the Snake River Road, call the Bureau of Land Management's Baker Resource Area at 541-523-6391.

Sumpter Dredge

Not long ago in the old Sumpter Valley, a mechanical beast the size of an apartment building spent its days plodding along the stream beds, eating the valley floor. As it dug itself ever deeper into the earth, it gobbled soil and guzzled river, and then spewed rubble out behind. But it was only doing it's job, for this beast was a dredge. And its job was digging gold.

Even though this dredge's days as a gold digger ended four decades ago, its history is still intact, for today it stands as the centerpiece of Oregon's newest state park—the Sumpter Valley Dredge State Heritage Area, located 30 miles west of Baker City. If you drive that stretch of road to the park, then you'll see what a dredge can do.

After you sweep past the juniper-crowned hills standing round and brown against a blue sky, past the basalt cliff sides wedging the Powder River into its shaded canyon, past the pine-clad slopes flanking the Elkhorn Mountains, then you'll see it—the Sumpter Valley, humped up and spread over with piles of rock and miles of rubble, with the spewed out remains of the gold-digging dredge.

"A dredge is simply a machine, similar to a combine used for harvesting wheat, or a potato digger working in the field," writes Stephen Alford, a dredge historian. "Similar to how one pulls the potatoes out of the ground, a gold dredge also digs and pulls the gold bearing earth up into its belly to be digested, keeping the gold and spewing the waste out the back on a stacker."

To handle this digging and pulling, the 1,240-ton Sumpter Valley Dredge—which is more than 100 feet long and 50 feet wide, and which was powered by a 250 horsepower electric motor connected to a 12-mile, 23,000-volt line—had 72 buckets, each able to dig a quarter yard of ground at a bite, then wash it down with 3,000 gallons of water per minute. This meant that every clanking minute of every working day the dredge could dig and dump 25 buckets, which added up to more than 9,000 cubic yards per day, or the equivalent of 1,000 dump truck loads.

Every year, the dredge dug another 100 acres of valley floor and river bed as deep as 30 feet. From the 1930s to the 1950s, with time out for World War II, this dredge's buckets ate earth, spewed rock, and found gold—$4.5 million worth at a time when its value was $35 per ounce. And because it was the third—and largest—dredge to work the Sumpter Valley, the results were devastating.

"[The] dredge converts lush grassland into useless rubble," reported a 1953 issue of *The Oregonian.* "Mountains of rubble from dredge tailings extend for miles as a result of dredging since 1913."

Although some people at the time worried about the destruction of river and farmland, the gold and the jobs it provided kept the dredges operating. One estimate puts the total value of dredge-dug gold in the valley at $10 million. The net profit, however, was much smaller; one estimate calculates that the Sumpter Valley Dredge, with a daily operating cost of $700, needed to find $1,000 of gold per day to make money. But when the operation's cost finally exceeded its profits, the last dredge shut down. (The first two were dismantled for parts in the 1920s.)

Abandoned in 1954, the Sumpter Valley Dredge sank to the bottom of the shallow pond it had dug for itself. And there it sat for more than 30 years. The hull and deck soaked, the timbers and planks rotted.

Then in 1985 a group of citizens and businesses from the nearby town of Sumpter had an idea. As a way to spark tourism and boost the economy, they would resurrect the dredge as a state park. "We had bus tours coming by to look at the dredge even in her dilapidated condition," says a woman named Teri, who has run The Gold Post store and museum in Sumpter for the past 12 years. "So we knew it had potential."

Teri credits the late Jerry Myers, who subsequently became the town's mayor, with spearheading the effort and then coordinating the project with Oregon Parks. "He knew about Sumpter's history," she says, "and he understood what the town had to offer."

Even though the group had ideas, energy, and leadership, it had no money. So it formed Friends of the Sumpter Valley Dredge and raised $350,000 in grant money—the same amount required to build the dredge in 1935. In 1995, the dredge's restoration began; in 1998, 13 years after those first meetings, it opened for public tours.

The dedication ceremony marking that grand opening featured a group of former dredge workers who reminisced about the working conditions aboard the old machine—of three crews of three men each working eight hour shifts around the clock, of getting only Christmas Day and the Fourth of July off during the year, of working in temperatures as cold as 42 degrees below zero, and of earning roughly a dollar per hour in the years after World War II.

The grinding, freezing dredge of these men's working lives seems to be a world away from the one the Oregon Parks and Recreation Commission calls "an important historic and cultural resource that links Oregon's pioneering past with settlement and development."

Nevertheless, when you step aboard the dredge you'll still find the smell of grease and the hulking, hovering presence of steel in the winches and cables and buckets, in the welds and bolts and rivets holding together the ladder and spud and stacker. Out behind the dredge are the signs of its work—the tailings piled along the Powder River.

To see these, take the Dredge Loop Trail, a half-mile gravel path that is decorated with buckets and cables, picnic tables and drive shafts. After a short stroll along the river, a fork in the path lets you take either the Ridge Trail, which climbs to a hilltop dividing two gullies that are thick with cottonwoods, willows, and pines; or the Loop Trail, which skirts the edge of town, passing the backyards of cabins before leading back to the dredge.

Even though it stands today as our newest state park, the Sumpter Valley Dredge needs more money and requires more work before it is completed. Yet even in its unfinished state, the dredge still serves as a monument not only to a time gone by, but also to a community that saw in its past a hope for its future.

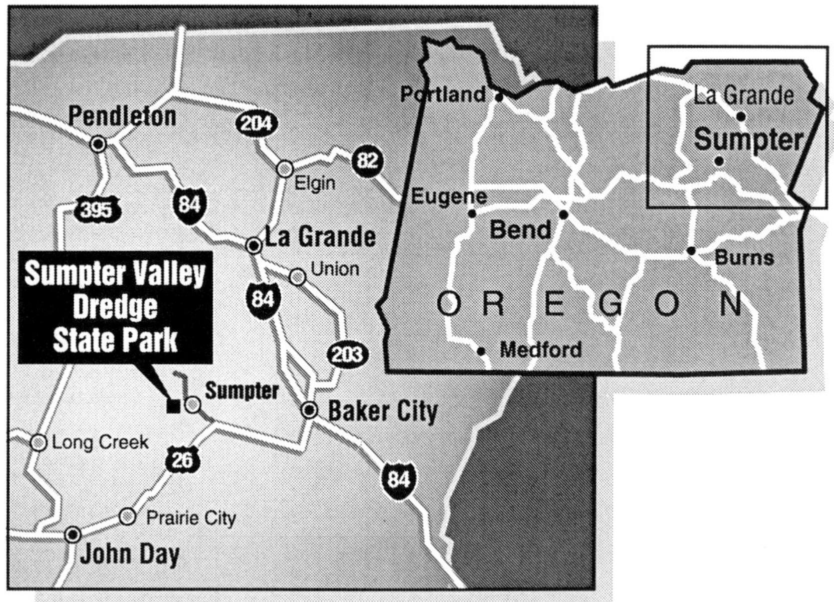

Where to Go

•From Baker City, take Highway 7 for 26 miles to the Sumpter junction.

When to Go

•The park is open May 15 to September 15 from 9:00 am until 4:00 pm, and September 16 to October 31 from 9:00 am until 3:00 pm. It is, however, closed Tuesdays and Wednesdays.

Things to Know

•The first Sumpter dredge operated from 1913 to 1924; the second, from 1915 to 1923; and the third, from 1935 to 1942 and then again from 1945 to 1954.

Who to Contact

•For more information about the park, call the Park Ranger at 541-894-2486.

•For information about Sumpter, call Teri at The Gold Post, 541-894-2362.

Swick Creek Trail

For more than 200 years they survived everything that people or nature threw at them—logging and fire, grazing and bugs, even Smokey the Bear. Now these ancient ponderosa pines, these testaments to age and endurance, stand near the mile-high summit of Highway 395, along the Swick Creek Old Growth Trail outside John Day, Oregon.

Think of forests east of the Cascades and you think of pines—the big-trunked (up to 180 feet tall and six feet thick), long-living (up to 500 years), light-loving, space-craving, yellow-bellied ponderosa pines. And the older they get, the more beautiful they grow. That's certainly true in this area, where the grass of Bear Valley meets the trees of Malheur National Forest, and where the pines were born before Lewis and Clark even considered a West coast excursion.

But what sets apart the Swick Creek Trail is not the age of the trees but the permanence of their home. "It's not a rare area as far as the trees are concerned," says Jaque (pronounced "Jackie") McConnell of the Malheur National Forest, "but it is an area that can't be disturbed by the multitude of activities that can take place in the general forest." Those activities can include grazing, logging, recreation, even land exchanges.

This desire to protect old-growth comes from the accelerating threat to Oregon's forests. When Europeans first settled the Northwest, ancient pines covered millions of acres, and much of the Blue Mountain region is said to have resembled a park. Then things changed.

"Over the past 80 years," says Oregon governor John Kitzhaber, "forest management policy, characterized by active fire suppression and harvesting of valuable old growth pine, has transformed these forests to...overstocked stands of young fir and pine, thousands of acres of dead and dying timber infested with insects, and an unacceptable risk of catastrophic fire."

Yet even after the U.S. Forest Service adopted dedicated old-growth as part of its forest plan in 1991, it still took four more years to find the funds necessary to build an interpretive site. "The purpose of the trail is to inform the public of the benefits of old growth," McConnell says. And because the trail actually consists of two connected paths, you have two ways to learn the lessons that old pines can teach.

The shorter route is a three-quarter mile "universal-access" trail (once called handicapped-access). Beginning at the parking lot, this needle-strewn, asphalt path is just wide enough for two people to stroll side-by-side, just long enough to give you a good gawk at

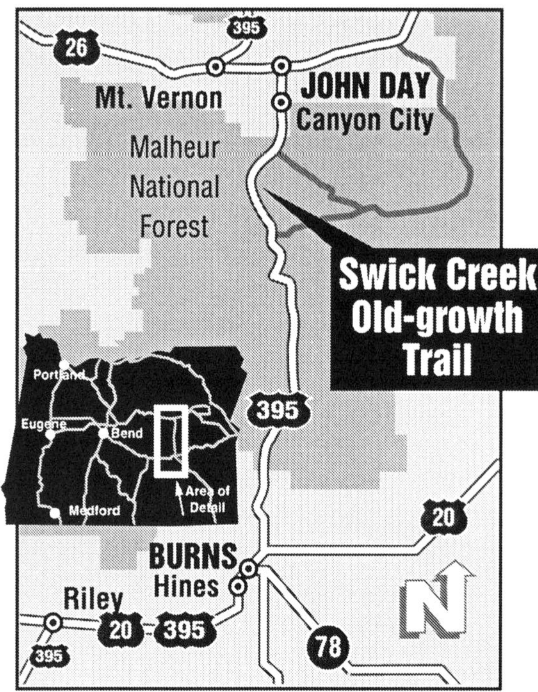

200 year old pines whose branches breathe the scent of pitch, and whose bark glows the color of burnished copper.

As the saying goes, "Old trees aren't necessarily big, and big trees aren't necessarily old." But here the trees are both old and big, and the Forest Service says it "is committed to maintaining significant areas of old growth."

Along the trail are interpretive signs telling you that white-headed woodpeckers nest and feed here, that wax currants provide browse and berries, that dead trees furnish habitat, and that rotting logs replenish the soil. Although the rumble of highway is near, you'll leave it behind after a 15 minute meander past sitting benches built by a local high school shop class and woodpiles left from trail clearings.

If you're interested in seeing more country, at about the mid-way point on this loop look for a side road straying from the asphalt. This is the beginning of the second path—the mile-and-a-half "native-surface" trail. Follow it, and you'll soon find yourself on the edge of a small meadow, where a brown fiberglass marker shows you the way to a wilder section of the forest.

The footpath edges past the meadow and heads into the timber, a land of ancient stands and logging scars, seedlings and slash, snags and stumps. (These stumps, mossy and charred, are filled with the debris of the ages—wood chips, rodent scat, grass starts, pine needles, bird droppings.)

Wandering past thickets, through meadows and up slopes, you'll scuff through duff and duck under moss. Scattered along the route are more sitting benches, which give you chances either to rest your feet or to stare off toward trees that were born about the time Thomas Jefferson wrote the Declaration of Independence, and were already a half century old when David Douglas, the Scottish botanist, named the tree for its heavy—or ponderous—wood.

Back on the ponderosa path, even an amateur scatologist will recognize the signs left by canine (probably coyote), bovine (maybe Hereford), and avian (certainly goose). But the droppings can be easier to identify than the trail. Unless you make the trek after a maintenance crew has passed through, you may find the path occasionally losing you. If that happens, here are some landmarks to keep in mind:

The halfway mark is an aspen grove where two benches sit; to the west, an old railroad grade steers you toward a broken fence line bordering a large, wet meadow; skirt the edge of the meadow and look for the fiberglass trail markers; if that fails, look for the

Where to Go

•The Swick Creek turnoff is on Highway 395, approximately eight miles north of Seneca and 15 miles south of Canyon City.

Things to Know

•The pine is the most common conifer both in the world (100 species) and in North America (30 species). Eight species are native to Oregon.

•David Douglas, who named the ponderosa, also named three other Oregon's pines—lodgepole, sugar, and western white.

•Oregon has two world-class ponderosas. Near Bend is one nine feet in diameter, and near Grants Pass is one 246 feet high. These are possibly the world's thickest and tallest, respectively. The state's oldest ponderosa lived for 726 years.

Who to Contact

•For more information, call the Malheur National Forest office in John Day at 541-575-1731.

"flag line," the red surveyor's ribbons that mark the cross-country ski route.

Did you follow that all right? (I didn't when I tried.) Don't worry, though, because you can't go far without running into a road—and sometimes the adventure is in the detour.

Besides, if you wait a while to visit Swick Creek, and if the Forest Service's plans for the area work out, you'll soon be able to follow a new course of interpretive signs, which will extend along the larger loop. These will explain some of the historical features of the area, including homesteading, railroading, and logging.

But for now, it's enough that places such as the Swick Creek Trail offer a route into a distant and different Oregon, where giant pines defied everything but time.

SOUTHEAST

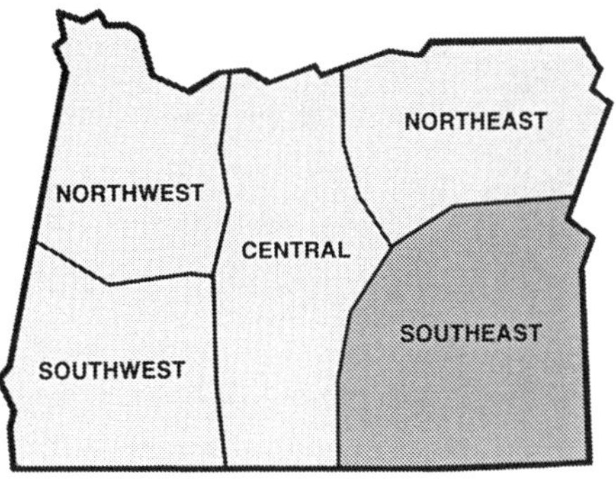

Diamond Loop

"History seemed to crowd right into the car with me," a traveler once wrote about his first tour of the Diamond Valley area in southeast Oregon. Whether the history is volcanic or human, whether you travel by bicycle or automobile, it's easy to feel that same nudge when you explore the high desert's Diamond Loop.

The entire Loop—one of Oregon's Back Country Byways—involves 75 miles of roads both paved and graveled, as well as more miles of spontaneous side trips and impulsive wanderings. For this reason, you might want to start by exploring a part that begins an hour's drive south of Burns at the town of Diamond.

This end-of-the-pavement town, named for an early settler's diamond-shaped brand, consists of a hotel, some houses, a row of 100 year old poplars, and the remains of stone buildings. Near the turn of the century it had a population of 50, and served as a supply center for the area's cattlemen, sheepherders, and camptenders. Evidently, it was a lively town.

"It became a common occurrence for the residents in the surrounding area to gather on a weekly basis for lively fiddle music, John Barleycorn, and occasional fisticuffs," a local historian wrote.

Even though the century-old Hotel Diamond is now the town's only business, its family-style meals have become the stuff of local legend. "They serve steak dinners on platters the size of garbage can lids," says Jack Zaring, a Coos Bay resident who tries to visit the hotel yearly.

But hold off on the vittles until you take the tour. Here's what to expect...

Diamond Valley

This is actually a loop within the Loop—a 13 mile route of half pavement and half gravel that circles one end of the valley. To begin from Diamond, head west on Grain Camp Road, past rocky slopes, willowy ditches, and scattered ranches. After less than six miles, you'll reach a junction where a paved road leads north. (Although some maps call this the Lava Bed Road, you probably won't see that name on signs.) Turn right, watch for muskrats and herons along the ditches, and travel the mile to North Diamond Loop Road. Here the pavement ends and the gravel begins.

This route runs along the edge that divides the basalt and sage of the uphill slopes from the haystacks and grass of the valley pastures. On one side you might find mule deer loafing among the boulders and valley quail scurrying toward the junipers; on the other, ranch dogs prancing or waddling out for a bark or a sniff.

But you'll find places where wild and tame join—geese and cranes grazing alongside cattle, bleached bones scattered across irrigated soil, tumbleweeds and boulders strewn along fields and fences. In fact, those boulders too large to move are part of the fences, serving as one-rock jacks that anchor posts and wire to volcanic ground. With Steens Mountain on the skyline for company, the gravel road steers you back to Diamond, back to pavement.

If you want to tackle a larger loop—a trip of approximately 28 miles, excluding side excursions—proceed to the Grain Camp-Lava Bed junction, but this time stay on the pavement, and in less than two miles you'll reach the entrance to Diamond Craters.

Diamond Craters

This area is for people with rocks in their heads, people who want to learn about the stuff the Earth pours and heaves out of itself to make soil and mountains, people who want to wander along volcanic rims or step through lava fields.

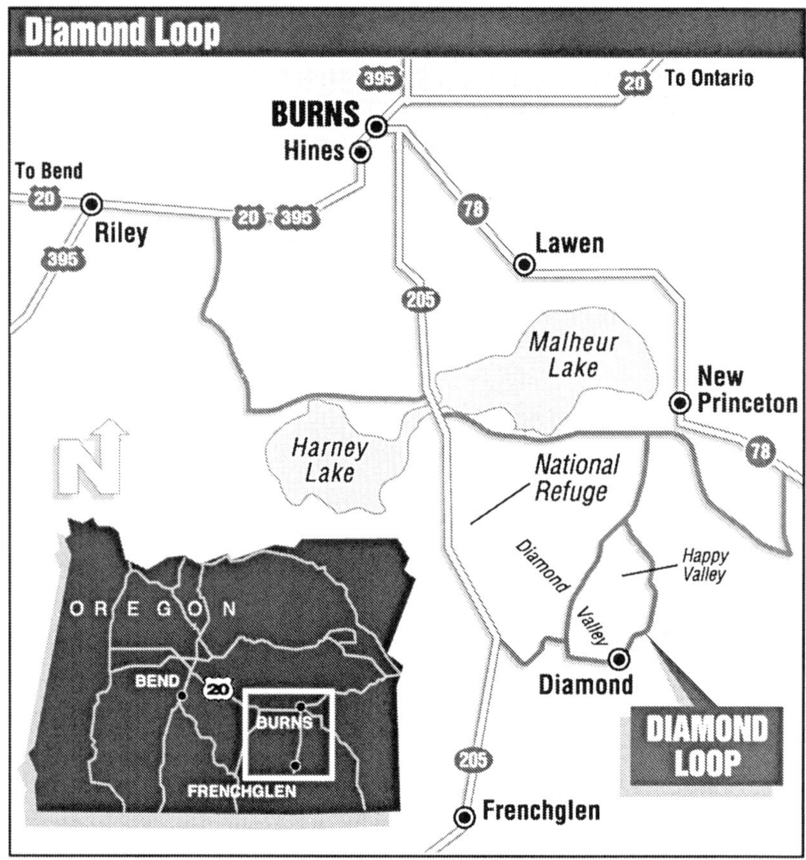

Called the "best and most diverse basaltic volcanic features in the United States," the Diamond Craters Outstanding Natural Area (ONA) consists of 17,000 acres of craters and vents, cones and tubes. And if you're willing to leave the pavement that hugs one edge of the ONA, you can walk through layers of time, step into a past when fire formed the land.

Perhaps the best side trip starts near the beginning of the ONA—at a turnout on the left-hand side of the road, next to a red cinder cone. This is Big Bomb Crater. From here, a gravel road leads west, penetrating approximately four miles into the heart of the ONA, taking you first to the nearby Lava Pit Crater (a shield volcano) and Red Bomb Crater (a thousand feet in diameter), then to the more distant East Twin and West Twin Craters (explosion craters), Dry Maar (a miniature "Hole in the Ground"), and the Central Crater Complex.

From the black or red rims of these formations, you'll see a land of grass, water, and distance; you'll find the signs of chukar, rabbit, and deer. "But you can't see anything man-made from up here," says a woman standing on the rim of Red Bomb Crater. Gazing at the stretch of land lying between volcanic fields and Steens Mountain snow, she says, "A good place to have a horse."

The mountain is a reminder that you're standing more than three quarters of a mile high, so the weather here can change in moments from grass-stirring breezes to rock-pelting rain. But it's one of the chances you take when you walk through time.

Back on the pavement, you'll find less than nine road miles of the Diamond Craters left, including a hilltop overlook of the area's northern half. After this, the journey leaves behind rocks and leads into grassland. Cowboy country.

Happy Valley

Yes, Virginia, cowboys still ride horses, still rope steers, still herd cows—at least they still do in Happy Valley. An Oregon landmark

Where to Go

•The Diamond turnoff is 42 miles south of Burns on Highway 205 (between mileposts 40 and 41). From here, Diamond is 12 miles west.

What to Expect

•Don't believe the brochures that tell you Diamond has gas and groceries. It doesn't.

Things to Know

•George McCoy named Happy Valley, saying that the settlers there "were so hospitable and happy."

•"Aroused by loss of treaty lands to white settlers," says a line from Oregon history, "Bannock Indians resorted to war in May 1878—the last major uprising in the Pacific Northwest and the most severe in this area..."

Who to Contact

•For more information, call BLM's District Office in Burns, 541-573-5241.

and a historical connection between the valley's cowboy past and present is the round barn of legendary cattle king Pete French.

Built with juniper tree trunk posts and beams in 1883, the 100-foot diameter barn stands a mile from the junction of the Lava Bed and Happy Valley Roads. Inside the barn, a circular stone wall forms a 20-foot wide runway between it and the wall; this was where French's cowboys broke horses during the winter.

Meanwhile, back at the ranch—er, junction—the Happy Valley Road takes you on a curving climb through open country, surrounding you with sage and grass while pointing you south toward the mountains. After about six miles, you'll find an edge-of-the-rim view of Smyth Reservoir, which was named for two local heroes of the 1878 Bannock-Paiute uprising.

"If heaven is a place for men like Jim Bowie, David Crockett and James Travis," a local historian wrote more than three decades ago, "then as sure as the sun sets in the west, George and John Smyth are up there with them." According to local legend, the Smyths—outnumbered ten to one—killed 30 warriors before their house was burned down with them still inside. Yet even then, "the men died shooting to the last."

Past the reservoir, juniper and sage replace fences and pastures, and you'll see more deer than cattle. In less than three miles, you'll reach a summit, pass the turnoff to the Kiger mustang viewing area, and then start a steep downhill run along the Diamond Grade, which gives you a long view of the landscape while leading you back to Diamond.

But after your journey, you might sense a change in the place, might feel the nudging push of history that grabs hold after you've wandered through this land of volcanoes and cowboys.

Four Rivers Cultural Center

Before it was a political trend, a popular movement, or even a word in the dictionary, multi-culturalism was a way of life around Ontario, Oregon, where the history of the area's five cultures join the same way the valley's four rivers do. In fact, that's the idea behind Ontario's Four Rivers Cultural Center, which advertises itself as a place "Where rivers converge and cultures unite."

The rivers are the Malheur, Owyhee, Snake, and Payette; the cultures are the Northern Paiute, European, Basque, Japanese, and Hispanic. Because of this mix, around here they not only put an "American" suffix on a lot of labels—Native American, European American, etc.—but also emphasize that the area is "a cultural melting pot that's been simmering for nearly 200 years."

The idea for Four Rivers began with Ontario's Japanese community, especially those who spent World War II in internment camps, a confinement that some call "the most serious violation of constitutional rights in U.S. history." When Japanese Americans later sought an apology, President Reagan responded in 1988 by signing legislation that expressed the nation's regrets and offered $20,000 to each former internee. According to one official, the donations of these "redress checks" became the "seed money" that gave the center its start.

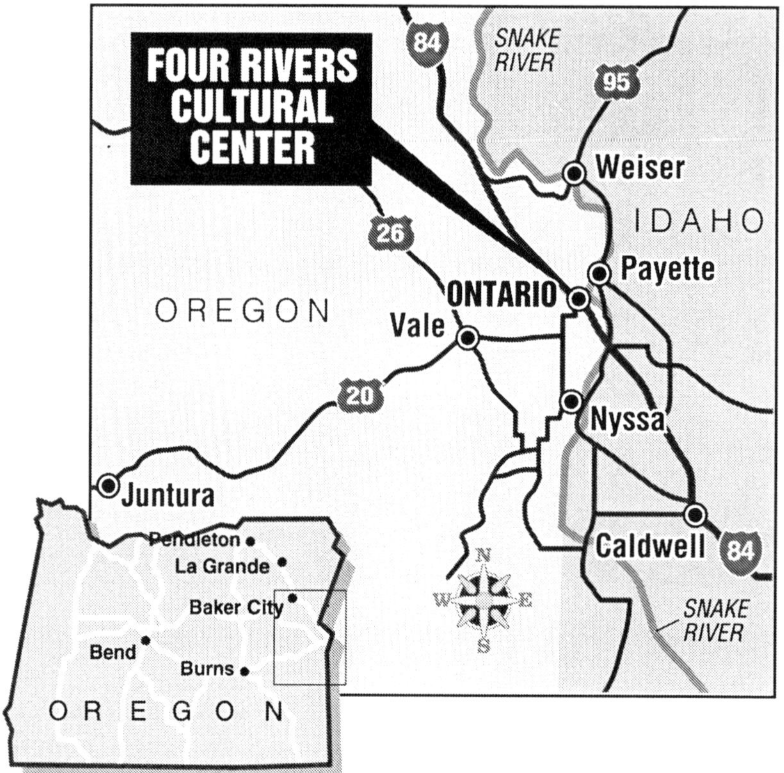

The heart of the center is its 10,000 square foot museum, which tells the story of the valley's five cultures. A tour through the museum's two galleries gives you a local view of the march of people through Western history—Native Americans, beaver trappers, gold miners, cattle ranchers, sheepherders, war refugees, and farm workers.

The beginning of this parade is the museum's Northern Paiute camp, complete with reed boat, duck decoys, and mat house. Once scattered through more than 70,000 square miles of the Great Basin, the Northern Paiute may have lived in this area for as long as 10,000 years. In fact, Paiute legends refer to a time before the Cascade Mountains formed, which means their ancestors lived here when camels and mammoths roamed eastern Oregon. In this region of the four rivers lived the Agaidika, the Salmon Eaters. (Bands were named for an important food source in their area.)

Running through the museum's story of the Paiute are the trappers of the 1820s and 1830s, the emigrants of the 1840s and 1850s, the miners and soldiers of the 1860s, and the cowboys and wars of the 1870s. But even though the Northern Paiute are honored in the museum, you probably won't find their descendants in the community.

"It's the same old story," says a former Ontario resident visiting the museum. "Cattlemen and homesteaders wanted the Indians' land, so politicians wrote up the treaties, and soldiers sent them to the reservation. As far as I know, the Paiutes never returned."

In spite of this conflict over land ownership, the first emigrants passing through were unimpressed with the area. "The plains smoked with dust and death," Thomas Farnham, an 1839 Oregon Trail emigrant, wrote about it. "This is a barren, God forsaken country, fit for nothing but to receive the footprints of the savage and his universal associate the coyote."

But as the museum shows, many who followed didn't share Mr. Farnham's view, and "Ontario emerged from sand clouds," according to an early settler. Although the town's population in 1893 was only 100, roads and bridges, ferries and stages, trains and

Where to Go

•From Interstate 84 take Exit 376; from either Highway 20 or 26, follow the signs to Treasure Valley Community College (TVCC) and the Four Rivers Cultural Center.

When to Go

•The center is open daily—except holidays—from 10 AM until 6 PM, Mountain Time.

Things to Know

•Ontario began with construction of the Oregon Short Line railroad, which was completed in 1883. The town was named for Ontario, Canada, the birthplace of one of its early settlers.

•"The hardest thing to do is go out and fight against those who you know are in the right," General George Crook said about the Paiute and Bannock war of 1878. Even so, Crook offered the Paiute "Peace or Death." They chose peace and moved to the Malheur Reservation.

Who to Contact

•For more information, call Four Rivers at 1-888-211-1222.

wagons—some among the museum's exhibits—began moving supplies and people into the area.

Among these were the Basque, whose homeland is the Pyrenees mountains between France and Spain. In the early part of this century, thousands of Basques came to work as sheepherders on the open range of the far West. It was "the great era of western sheep raising" when sheep outnumbered cows by a ratio of 7-1.

Then came the farmers, who wrote another chapter of local history when they figured out how to pull water from distant Lake Owyhee. "A vast green oasis is due to rise phoenix like from the dun gray of the sage, " said a 1929 article in the *Idaho Statesman,* referring to the irrigation project that began during the Depression, and that makes today's Treasure Valley "the most intensive, diversified row crop farming area in the state." In the museum, you can even take a stroll through one of the irrigation pipes.

Perhaps the most moving exhibits concern the Japanese, who were classified as enemy aliens following the bombing of Pearl Harbor. Given seven days to leave their homes, 120,000 Japanese immigrants and their American born children were moved to "relocation centers."

The closest center to Ontario was Idaho's Minidoka Internment Camp, where 9,000 people lived in 500 barracks surrounded by barbed wire and guard towers. A family's furnishings consisted mainly of a potbelly stove, some cots, and one light bulb. Even though temperatures ranged from 20 degrees below zero in winter to 115 above in summer, the physical deprivation wasn't always the most difficult struggle of those years.

"So much I left behind," said internee Teru Watnabe, "but the most valuable thing I lost was my freedom." When they regained their freedom after the war, some Japanese families remained in the area and began working the newly irrigated farmland.

At the same time, Hispanic families began arriving, and a second gallery leads you through a background of their history and heritage. You'll also have the chance to visit a replica internment camp barracks, a Paiute reservation cabin, a Basque boarding house, and a "European-American" kitchen typical of the 1950s.

"It's just like Mom's kitchen!" says a woman poking around the 1955 reproduction. "Mom wouldn't have known what it meant to be called a European American, but that's her kitchen anyway, right down to the mixer and the cross-stitch." She reads the message of the cross-stitch hanging on the kitchen wall—"To a Friend's House the Road is Never Long."

In its first year after opening in 1997, the museum saw 13,000 visitors pass through its doors. "We're staying busy," says Richard Nielsen, the center's facilities director. He adds, however, that the center encourages even more people to make the museum a vacation destination. After all, in a land coveted by so many for so long, it might be worth your time to see what all the fuss is about.

Malheur Crossing

Across the Snake River they came, struggling against deep water and swift currents. "It was a very long tedious task," Oregon Trail emigrant Martha Hill Gillette wrote about her family's 1853 river crossing near Fort Boise, "and when finished, men and stock would both be almost exhausted."

Their fatigue was almost heartbreaking. By the time they reached Fort Boise, a Hudson Bay fur post which stood where the Boise River enters the Snake, emigrants had trudged through 1,600 miles of plains and mountains and deserts; they were low on money, supplies, and strength. But they still had plenty of Trail left. More than 400 miles of it. "But through it all," Martha Hill Gillette wrote, "I heard no word of grumbling."

To get a feel for both the land they crossed and the hardships they faced, perhaps the best way to travel the Trail through Oregon today is in the same direction the pioneers did, starting at the Snake River crossing near the town of Nyssa.

Located 13 miles south of Ontario on Highway 201, Nyssa is a farm community. In fact, the drive there takes you through some of the richest farmland in Oregon, a land tilled for crops and ditched and channeled for irrigation, a land of brown and blue, of soil and sky. At the edge of Nyssa, you'll find acres of farm implements, a crop of threshers and balers and discs.

Rounding the corner on Highway 201 (follow the Lake Owyhee sign), you'll see in the distance one of the sights that welcomed emigrants to Oregon—the rims of the Owyhee country, with its plateaus and benches and draws. And down the road near Milepost 5, you'll find the kiosk that marks their crossing of the Snake River. Near here, the emigrants stepped into what would become the state of Oregon.

The river, however, proved difficult. It confused livestock, capsized wagons, and drowned emigrants. Luckily for the wagon trains, local Indians hired out to help with the crossing. "There are indians who swim the river from morning till night. It is fun for them," wrote an 1853 emigrant.

Although the river is too distant to see from here, the interpretive area contains markers showing where the wagons rolled after leaving the Snake. Unfortunately, it can be easy to lose the Trail after this because road and map don't always line up. If you find this to be the case, head a few highway miles south to the Owyhee Grocery, a building fronted with red stone and petrified wood, arched doors and windows.

"I've seen lots of people with those maps," says the man behind the store's counter. "And they get lots of people turned around." To straighten you out, he'll point you west, toward Lytle Boulevard, which follows the Trail to Vale, showing some of the clearest wagon ruts in the state.

Stone markers along the roadside show you the wagon route through what emigrants called Keeney Pass, named for Jonathan Keeney, a former mountain man who traveled with Jim Bridger, and later guided his family and others to Oregon.

His route leads you through a dusty hollow spotted with homes and cows and cornfields, then into hills covered green and white with sagebrush and alkali. This is a gentle road through a harsh land, a dusty and thirsty land, where the wind can sandpaper your eyes.

"...o dear if we were only in Willamette valley or where ever we are going for I am tired of this," Agnes Stewart Warner wrote during her 1853 trip through here.

From the Snake to the Malheur was 15 waterless miles, one dust-choked, sun-baked day. To get a perspective of this journey,

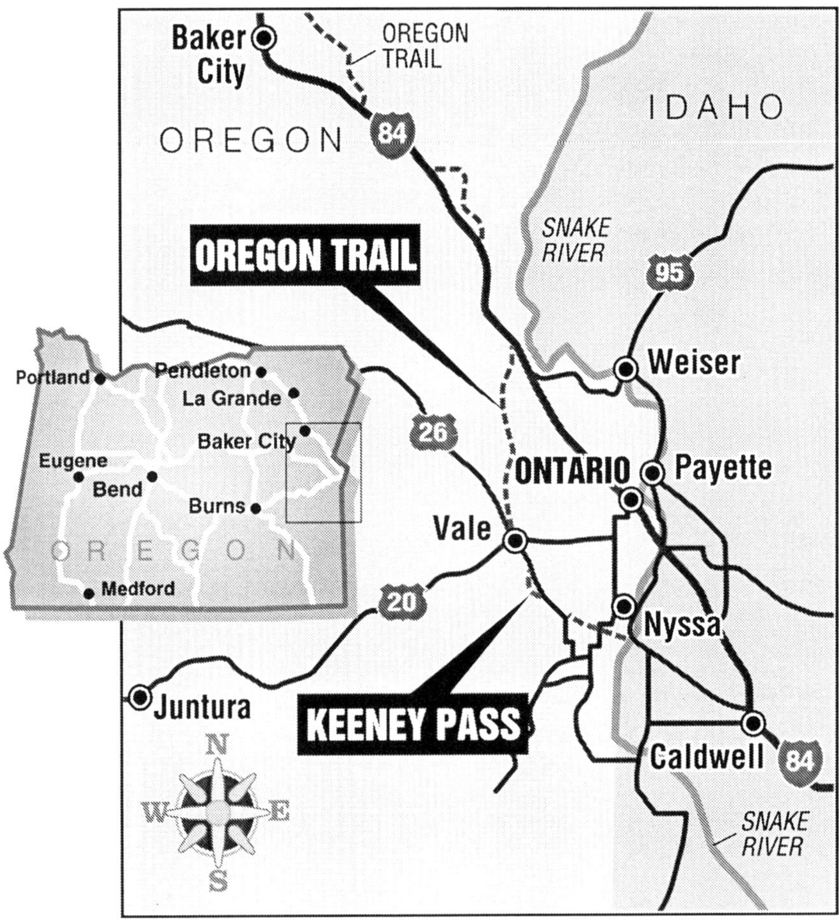

pull into the BLM's Keeney Site. Here you'll find interpretive signs, wagon ruts, and a footpath, which leads to an overlook showing you the land of the one day journey between rivers.

For a few yards, this walkway crosses the Trail. For a few moments, you cross paths with history, step in the ruts of wagons, and walk in the tracks of pioneers. Some things nearby would be strange to the emigrants—chukars, tumbleweeds, cattle guards, and zinging four wheelers rutting the hills. But others would be familiar—jackrabbits, ryegrass, sagebrush, and sandy slopes rolling to the horizon. Yet even more familiar would be the grave you'll find down the road on the outskirts of Vale.

"Died of Thirst August 9, 1852," says the marker on John Henderson's grave. "Unaware of Nearness of the Malheur River." A good story. The river is a few hundred yards from here. But a different marker explains that Mr. Henderson died of black measles. The burial site's importance, however, is as a symbol rather than a legend, for it represents the countless unmarked, unknown graves along the 2,000 mile route.

Sometimes called the "longest graveyard," the Trail claimed as many as 30,000 lives. That's one grave for every 100 yards between the Missouri and Willamette Rivers. Yet only a few hundred of these graves have been located. One reason for this was the pioneer practice of concealing graves against looters or predators by burying the dead on the trail; then as the wagons rolled over it, hoofs and wheels and feet trampled away any evidence of the site.

The site near Vale, however, not only marks John Henderson's burial, but also shows the character of his friends, for one man took the time to chisel Henderson's name into the rock that marked his grave. He must have done it during the rest the emigrants gave themselves after reaching the nearby river, where they could slake their thirsts and wash their clothes at Malheur Crossing.

"...just reached Malheur river and campt," says Amelia Knight's 1853 diary entry, "the roads have been very dusty, no water, nothing but dust and dead cattle all day..."

What Amelia Knight probably found was what explorer John C. Fremont described in 1843 as a river 50 feet wide and 18 inches

Where to Go

•To visit the site of old Fort Boise, follow Highway 201 from Nyssa to Parma, Idaho.

•Vale offers a self-guided walking tour of its murals and historic buildings.

Things to Know

•As the fur trade declined in the 1840s, so did Fort Boise. One emigrant described it as "that world renowned Spot of one miserable block house all going decay..."

•A local historian has traced the "Died of Thirst" legend connected to John Henderson's death to a story written by a Vale third grader.

Who to Contact

•For more information, call BLM's District Office in Vale, 541-473-3144.

deep, with a hot springs of 193 degrees. Near this place today is a mushroom plant and a grocery store, but the springs are still hot enough to make steam rise on a cool morning.

Although it provided a place to wash off the trail dust and gather some firewood, many found the area unappealing. One emigrant described it as "so rugged, so dreary, and so exceeding sterile that it cannot...yield anything worthy of consideration to the support of human life..." Others, however, disagreed—especially when gold was discovered nearby in the early 1860s.

That's when Jonathan Keeney returned, started a ferry near the Snake River Crossing, and built Vale's first cabin near the bank of the river. Even though that cabin is gone and Vale has grown to become the Malheur county seat, this town of 1,500 people holds on to its past.

Evidence of this is as close as town, where the walls of the buildings display murals depicting the theme, "Born and raised on the Oregon Trail." In this outdoor art gallery, the sides of at least a dozen stores, shops, and agencies show trappers and pioneers, soldiers and settlers making their pictorial journeys along the venerable trail.

Like the emigrants who stopped at the nearby crossing, you might want to take some time here—at this end of a hard day's journey between rivers, where pioneers began their march across Oregon.

Malheur Refuge

Daybreak. Oregon's high desert. The eastern sky unfolds in one slow blink, and from beneath a brow of shaggy red clouds comes a pale gaze of light. The Malheur National Wildlife Refuge rouses, its voice vibrating with the chirps and warbles and whistles of birds. In spring, this wetland is a world of wings and water, where a sagebrush ocean sprawls toward a basalt-broken horizon, and a journey through the heart of it has been the stuff of adventure for countless explorers—especially for those who have seen its birds.

"The sedges were full of birds, the tules were full of birds, the skies were full of birds," wrote a man who traveled through the region in the early years of this century. "I was beside myself at the sight—at the sound—at the thought that such wildlife could still be anywhere upon the face of the earth, to say nothing of finding it within the borders of my own land."

Indeed, the bird life of the refuge, which is located 32 miles south of Burns, defines the place. Covering approximately 185,000 acres, almost 290 square miles, Malheur is a major nesting, feeding, and staging area for more than 300 species of birds moving between their northern breeding areas and their southern wintering grounds along the Pacific Flyway.

Sometimes described as a lopsided T—with the T's top running 37 miles from the shore of Malheur Lake in the east and through the Double O Ranch to the west, and its stem stretching 41 miles from the refuge headquarters in the north to Frenchglen in the south—the refuge includes Malheur, Mud, and Harney Lakes as well as the Blitzen River Valley. And the story of the refuge follows many characters through many stages.

First on the scene were the Paiute Indians, who lived in this part of the Great Basin for more than 100 centuries. The first white men didn't show up until 1826, when Peter Skene Ogden rode through at the head of a Hudson Bay Company beaver-trapping brigade. The beaver trappers were followed by gold miners, who spread the word about the valley's sparkling stream and its lush grass. Next came the cattlemen, who came looking for that water and feed; then the soldiers, who chased out the Paiutes; and finally the settlers, who claimed the Indian's land. By the time things settled down, almost the entire Blitzen River Valley was owned by cattle baron Pete French, one of the first Californians to buy up Oregon real estate. In this case, 132,000 acres of it.

Starting with his entrance into the Blitzen Valley in 1872 and lasting until his shooting death in 1897, French worked his P Ranch into a cattle empire that stretched from the Blitzen River headwaters in the snow fields of Steens Mountain, to the river's mouth along the shore of Malheur Lake. And in-between was the Blitzen-watered desert oasis that French dredged, drained and dammed, turning marshes and ponds into hayfields and pastures. Soon herds of cattle and horses replaced flocks of waterfowl and shorebirds.

"He had grain growing where the ducks and geese once fed," *The Oregonian* reported, "and the fields he had taken from the aquatic birds were yielding 10,000 tons of hay each autumn."

It was the age of Oregon's old West, a time of cattle drives, Indian wars, and land feuds. But as the West settled down and homesteaders replaced cattle kings, it became the time of the plume hunter—men who slaughtered swans, egrets, grebes, and other birds for their feathers, which were used to decorate women's hats. The trumpeter swan was hit especially hard, and by the beginning of this century some authorities were predicting its extinction.

"A swan seen at any time of the year in most parts of the United States is the signal for every man with a gun to pursue it," wrote one ornithologist of the time, "and the trumpetings that were once heard over the breadth of a great continent...will soon be heard no more."

Other pressures on the birds came from the settlers who killed them for food and diverted their water for irrigation. As a result, the marshes began to wither and the birds to vanish. This situation led President Theodore Roosevelt to establish the Lake Malheur reservation in 1908. Through the years, as ranchers and settlers quit the desert, more land was added to the refuge, the habitat was restored, and the birds—including the swans—returned.

"For what Pete French sought to take from the ducks and the geese, the swans and pelicans, the herons, egrets, and the many other aquatic birds, now has been restored," *The Oregonian* reported. "Swamp again is swamp. Lake is lake." Yet those swamps and lakes are the work of refuge managers, not Mother Nature.

Because it's part of the Great Basin, the streams of the Malheur Refuge have no outlet to the sea; they flow into a low basin, form shallow lakes, and then begin to evaporate. Because of this, water levels fluctuate widely. With enough snowfall, Harney and Malheur Lakes flow together to form a vast, shallow inland sea of over 140 square miles. But in dry years, that changes.

"[Malheur Lake] has ranged from 60,000 to 500 acres in size," says a 1963 issue of the *Burns Time-Herald*. "Even during years of high water, its deepest parts rarely exceeded six feet, but in years of drought, such as occurred in the early 1930s, it was possible to drive a car across the dry lake bed."

To stabilize the water supply, over 100 miles of dikes and 200 miles of canals control stream flows and pond levels to meet the birds' nesting and feeding needs. The result is a refuge system famous for the numbers and diversity of its wildlife.

"These are not your common backyard feeder kinds of birds," says a woman peering through a pair of binoculars at one of the refuge's numerous marshes.

She's right, for this is the home of grebes, curlews and avocets, of egrets, herons and ibis, of tundra swans, sandhill cranes and snow geese—so many birds of so many species that at times the air and the water swirl and shimmer with the flutter of wings and the gabble of voices. And because this place is for the birds, much of the refuge is closed to the public, especially during the nesting season.

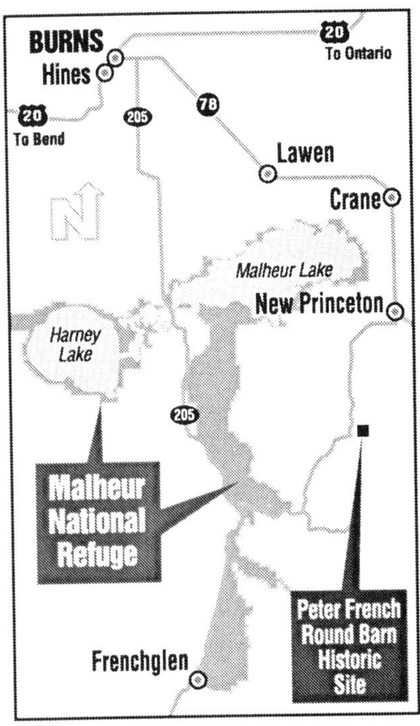

One route, however, remains open throughout most of the year—the Center Patrol Road, a 42 mile stretch of gravel that runs the length of the Blitzen Valley, through the grasslands and past the waterways that lie between refuge headquarters and the town of Frenchglen.

When traveling the road, the refuge managers recommend that you "go slowly. When you stop, turn off your engine and get out of your car; free yourself from that machine. Listen to the refuge sounds—the birds, water, wind, leaves, rustling grasses, insects; REALLY LISTEN! Watch the horizon, look for movements near water, smell the sage. Feel the weather. It's time to become a part of your world."

If you follow this advice in spring, you'll probably find that this world has the feel of forever to it, reaching far beyond the Indians, the trappers, the cowboys, the soldiers and the settlers who were once part of the Blitzen River Valley.

"It's one of those places where time doesn't matter," says the woman with the binoculars, now watching a white spangled cloud of snow geese whirl across a blue sky. "These birds have been making this migration forever."

Where to Go

•Refuge headquarters is located approximately 32 miles southeast of Burns.

When to Go

•Populations of ducks, geese, and cranes reach their peaks in March and April; shorebirds and songbirds in May.

What to Expect

•Be prepared for temperature extremes, gravel roads, and summer mosquitoes. ("From mid May through August," says one visitor, "the area is a refuge for trillions of mosquitoes.")

•Camping is permitted at four sites adjacent to the refuge.

Things to Know

•Pete French was shot and killed by Ed Oliver, a homesteader who had a running feud with French. But the jury in the 1898 trial acquitted Oliver, saying he had killed in self defense.

Who to Contact

•For more information, call refuge headquarters at 541-493-2612.

Sagehen Hill

So there you are, rolling across the desert between Bend and Burns, watching the alkali twirling into dust devils and the sagebrush scratching against barbed wire; the kids stare wide-eyed as the speedometer needle flutters toward 80, and the dog moans its car sickness from the back seat. The road seems endless. So does the Beach Boys tape. Time for a break? Then look for milepost 114—Sagehen Hill.

Located approximately 18 miles west of Burns, the rest area at Sagehen Hill holds more than a restroom; it's also home to a half-mile nature trail that takes you to the top of a knoll and shows you a long stretch of Harney County's desert world. To find it, wander around to the back side of the restrooms and look for the sign marking the trailhead.

The first thing you might notice about the trail is that you have it to yourself; that's because it's little known and seldom used, and if you step deeply enough into this land of basalt and sagebrush and sky, of stinging winds and gnarled junipers, you'll hike in relative solitude, leaving behind the asphalt whoosh and buzz of Highway 20, while learning about the desert world you've been driving through at better than a mile a minute.

The first lesson concerns the stuff you've been staring at mile after mile through the windshield—sagebrush. The walk begins in a patch of it—big sagebrush, one of the high desert's most widespread and important shrubs. Growing throughout eastern Oregon on approximately 20 million acres—more than 30,000 square miles, almost a third of the state's total land area—this silver leafed sage sets its roots in relatively deep soil, grows as tall as 12 feet, and serves as either cover or food for deer, pronghorns, and elk.

Past the sagebrush is the second mainstay of Oregon's high desert—the western juniper. The one hunkered here has probably been growing from the grit and rock of this spot of desert for generations. Because junipers can live longer than 1,600 years, this one should have a long life ahead of it. Even so, it's branches may have been shading the deer and its berries feeding the birds long before Highway 20 was even a wagon road.

At the juniper, pass through a turnstile and follow a dirt path uphill, through the fragrance of sagebrush and the waver of bunchgrass, past a lightning-hit tree and onto a ledge of volcanic rubble. The scraps of basalt strewn on the ground are the leftovers from an ancient lava flow, which cooled, contracted, and then cracked along the small fault you cross as you climb the slope to the top of the hill.

Once on top, you'll find the view expanding, opening to a world of a desert basin (Harney Valley to the east) and a glacier-carved mountain (Steens Mountain to the southeast). You'll also find the highway noise dimming. "It's so quiet here," says a woman along the trail with her Labrador retriever. "Almost silent."

Broken only occasionally by the sound of wind, jets, or robins, that silence seems to follow you along the trail and across the hilltop, where deer-browsed junipers grow, the lower branches stripped during hard winters of deep snow. Sharing this land with the deer is a band of 30 to 60 wild horses that had their beginning at a 96,000 acre wild horse management site near Palomino Buttes, which is visible to the south. (It was named for the palomino horses that nearby ranchers once raised.)

As you loop around the crest, stepping along with the hollow clunk of rock underfoot, you'll see another line of hills rippling the horizon to the west—the silhouettes of Wagontire Mountain, named for a wheel that once lay on its north slope, said to have come from an emigrant wagon burned by Indians; Squaw Butte, site of Oregon State University studies in rangeland grazing; and Glass Butte, an important source of obsidian for the bands of Northern Paiutes who lived here for 13,000 years.

Although at this point you will have seen how rugged this wind-scraped, scree-scattered land can be, nearby is evidence of yet another of the desert's harsh elements—a lightning-exploded juniper, its trunk split into layers and peeled like a banana. The resulting fire was one of 50 per year in the Burns BLM district, which sees about 20,000 acres burned each year. But as far as the desert is concerned, that's probably not enough.

The problem began, says an Oregon State University range scientist, when grazing began in this area in the 1870s. Then cattle and sheep ate the grass that once spread the wildfires. As a result, more young junipers survived, even as settlers were cutting the old junipers for fences and houses. Now the region faces an overpopulation of young trees—97 percent of junipers on the high desert are less than 100 years old—that suck the soil of water, leaving the nearby sagebrush and grasses to die of thirst.

But for this lightning-split juniper curling its charred limbs along the rimrock of Sagehen Hill, its drinking days are over. It does, however, still serve as a drooping gateway to the downhill trek, which first gives you a view of the Blue Mountains, then takes you through the kind of low sagebrush favored by pronghorns and sage grouse, and finally leads you out beneath the shade of another generations-old juniper.

At this tree you might want to stop and take a seat on the saw-gouged bench, for soon you'll be back to the whine of traffic and the hum of tires, the wagging speedometer needle and the endless gash of asphalt splitting the desert. But when it comes time to hit the road again, you'll probably find your view of the desert changed because after you've seen it from the top of Sagehen Hill, it won't ever look quite the same again.

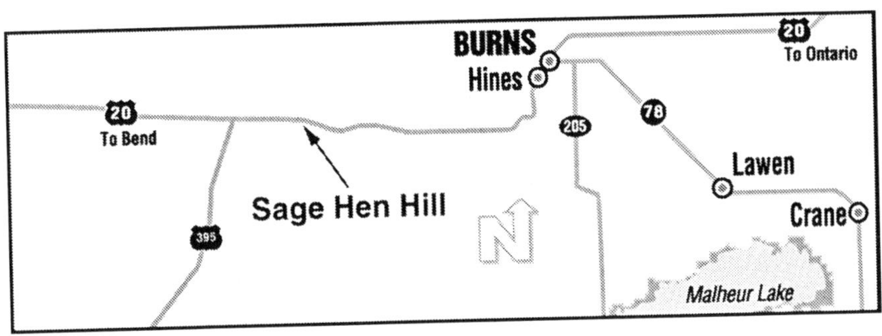

Where to Go

•Sagehen Hill is located near milepost 114 on Highway 20, approximately 18 miles west of Burns.

What to Expect

•An excellent trail guide is printed but not always available. Check the box at the trailhead.

•Although dogs are permitted on the trail, leashes are recommended so that pooch doesn't chase the wildlife.

Things to Know

•The trail is dedicated to the memory of Mark Hosket, a BLM employee who died in a 1986 airplane crash on Steens Mountain. Volunteers from Harney County built it as well as maintain it.

•The rest area at Sagehen Hill once displayed one of the world's few relatively clever restroom scrawls—"The earth is flat. Signed, the Class of 1491."

About the Author

Mark Highberger is a writer, a teacher, and an Oregonian. His novel *The Roar of the Bear* was published in 1994, and his articles and stories appear regularly in numerous regional and national publications. When not writing, he teaches in college courses and writers workshops throughout the Northwest. A lifelong resident of the state, Highberger lives with his wife and Labrador retriever in Wallowa, though he continues to wander the Oregon country.